Hall of Fame

How to Manage Financial Success as a
Professional Athlete

Benjamin F. Renzo, JD

iUniverse, Inc.
New York   Bloomington

iUniverse books may be ordered through booksellers or by contacting:

iUniverse
1663 Liberty Drive
Bloomington, IN 47403
www.iuniverse.com
1-800-Authors (1-800-288-4677)

Because of the dynamic nature of the Internet, any Web addresses or links contained in this book may have changed since publication and may no longer be valid. The views expressed in this work are solely those of the author and do not necessarily reflect the views of the publisher, and the publisher hereby disclaims any responsibility for them.

ISBN: 978-1-4401-9133-6 (sc)
ISBN: 978-1-4401-9134-3 (ebook)
ISBN: 978-1-4401-9135-0 (hc)

Printed in the United States of America

iUniverse rev. date: 5/20/2010

To my wife Linda and my children Ryley, Daniela, and Chase, who bring me so much joy and happiness. Without your support and love, I would not have had the opportunity to share my experiences in an effort to help others through this book. You will always remain the dearest part of my life.

Forward

Whether you're a professional athlete or entertainer, learning to successfully manage the issues surrounding new found wealth is critical in order to preserve and protect your earnings well into the future. However, success is not always defined in terms of financial reward. Success is also being a good spouse, parent, son or daughter, friend, community leader, partner, and/or mentor. This is why I spend my career helping professional athletes and entertainers manage their financial risk and business opportunities to a point where they will not only preserve and grow their financial success but will also contribute to their community and inspire others. The following chapters provide insight as to how financial success affects family relationships, one's spiritual journey and the importance and function of advisors- from investment advisors and attorneys to tax specialists-in guiding athletes throughout their careers and into retirement. I also review the basics of wealth management and how to analyze business opportunities and the role each advisor should play in order to secure an athlete's long-term financial success. Finally, I share the importance of charitable giving and the satisfaction of leaving a lasting legacy.

An athlete's transition from amateur to professional athletics and the years spent in the professional ranks are part of a transformational journey of growth and self-discovery. The promise of a multimillion-dollar income opens up a world of opportunities for athletes who, in the past, may have had limited access or experience with financial success. Coming into significant wealth often signals a changing of the tides, as fortune can have a profound effect on families, friends, and communities for generations to come.

But for young athletes, grasping the implications behind a high-profile career and all the money and fame that go along with it can be overwhelming. Additionally, managing newfound wealth is particularly daunting when an athlete is inexperienced and unfamiliar as to who to trust and hire in order to advise them regarding their short term and long term wealth planning needs.

These colliding forces can make daydreams of a perfect life seem out of reach, and the carefree attitude with which many professional athletes approach their financial planning and risk management have cost them substantial wealth, important relationships, and their identities.

That doesn't have to be the case.

Athletes must take an active approach to manage their careers and avoid potentially destructive temptations. With the emergence of social networking such as Twitter and Facebook, cell phone cameras/video, websites, sports talk radio/tv and instant worldwide communication, professional athletes and entertainers are under constant surveillance and live out their youth and mistakes in the court of public opinion. The bottom line is that coming into substantial wealth, celebrity and access without an experienced, independent, transparent and accessible advisory team will only make matters worse. I hope this book serves as a strong first step toward successfully managing the financial and personal opportunities afforded to professional athletes and entertainers. No one is perfect. However, success is primarily the result of a strong team and support system. Such support can be even more important during times when athletes and entertainers fail to live up to the expectations and values they embrace. I make sure my clients, who are blessed with wealth and access, know that they have the unique opportunity to positively affect many lives through their actions, charity and voice and they should use these gifts to promote a stronger, healthier and more productive community in an effort to leave a legacy that their family will honor for generations to come.

Contents

Chapter 1

How to Blend Fame and Money with Family

An athlete's financial success can have a substantial effect on his or her family members, presenting opportunities for parents, spouses, children, siblings, and other relatives to better themselves and have a positive effect on their communities. For the athlete, achieving that end requires not only careful wealth management and estate planning, but also relationship management when it comes to family members and close friends. Careful management will stabilize those personal relationships, insulate them from the effects of money and fame, and mitigate any risks that could threaten financial security.

"I think athletes need to understand that their relationships are going to change with every individual, including their parents, first and foremost, all the way down to that seventh cousin you never met," Former Tampa Bay linebacker Derrick Brooks says. "If you expect change, change shouldn't be that big of a surprise."[1]

Families are an invaluable source of love, support, and encouragement throughout life's many joys, triumphs, challenges, and heartaches. Unfortunately, families can also be a source of sadness, anger, or disappointment. Regardless of your past family experience, you can be assured that—for athletes on the brink of fame and fortune—families, if not managed correctly, can present roadblocks to one of life's biggest journeys and, in certain circumstances, jeopardize an athlete's financial security.

Each of us faces a broad range of struggles during the various chapters of our lives. These struggles are enhanced when you are in your early twenties and coming into millions of dollars. Money becomes the focal point of many family issues for athletes, and these issues are exacerbated by the constant threat that the money might be gone tomorrow. The entire family must determine how it can continue to relate and function in a positive way that is independent of the athlete's financial success on or off the field.

Family relationships present some of the most difficult challenges I face as an advisor for young athletes during their transitions from amateur to professional sports. My clients have been raised in a variety of family settings. Some grew up in families that have been overly involved in their careers and believe they have a significant stake in their success. The majority of my clients, however, grew up in single-parent households or with separated parents. Unfortunately, it is often easier for advisors to gain the trust and commitment of athletes and their families in the absence of a strong family support system. Without a strong and healthy support system, certain athletes are more likely to make rushed, uninformed decisions while putting their faith in people who will not keep their best interests in mind. Because of this, I stress the importance of checking the background and credentials of any potential advisors.

On the other hand, a strong family support system can also backfire and cause more harm than good when the expectations for an athlete are so high that the pressure of failure becomes too great. When this happens, the joy of competing no longer exists, and this can lead to resentment against those who love and support an athlete's success to a fault. Some families unknowingly force unhealthy expectations upon an athlete to the point that the athlete's entire identity within the family revolves around his potential ability to make a lot of money. Some family members, often unintentionally, hang their hopes on the athlete's future success, dreaming about what life will be like in five years when he's making $10 million a year—or so they hope.

For moms, dads, aunts, or uncles who spent their entire lives working tirelessly to provide a better life for an athlete, this success might equate to a new car, a new house, and a new lifestyle. Some may see the athlete's success as an opportunity for them to forget about their own failures in the past, or it may provide them a second chance to pursue a productive and meaningful life.

Suddenly, that family member is equally vested in the professional success of the athlete, putting pressure on him that is both subtle and powerful. Some athletes acknowledge that pressure and manage it constructively. For others, it becomes a burden that instigates family conflicts down the road. Regardless of their family background, young athletes come with diverse family problems and issues that must be dealt with up front in order to avoid misunderstandings, false expectations, or bad habits. The rules provided below will help athletes navigate potential problems and avert hard feelings.

Rule 1: Give back to your family, but set boundaries.

Upon signing their first pro contracts, many rookie athletes set out on their career paths with the intention of sharing their newfound wealth with family members. They feel an obligation to share their financial successes with loved ones and give back to those who provided love, support, and encouragement over the years. As an advisor, I support that objective, but I encourage clients to give back in a way that is constructive and emphasizes personal responsibility.

If there are certain occasions or situations where your family needs financial support, it is essential that you develop a carefully laid out plan that details how your support will be structured. Handing a blank check over to your parents or other family members once a month can bring unhealthy expectations, leading them to believe you will always be there for a handout. "If you lack a detailed plan and hand over sums of cash every month with no rules attached," Brooks says, "Family members will turn your financial gift into a weapon rather than an asset."[2]

Family members must understand the same reality that you have or will come to understand: *your playing days are limited, as is your multimillion-dollar team salary.* The money you earn as a professional athlete should last for decades, or perhaps for generations, with the help of a well-managed wealth plan and asset preservation strategy. Allowing your family to participate in your earnings without setting boundaries may severely jeopardize your long-term financial goals and alter your relationship with your family.

For Brooks, the guiding force in the early months and years of his career was fear—fear that he would somehow lose the money he had earned. Though he desperately wanted to provide his parents with financial assistance, fear made him extremely cautious about how he distributed his income.

Brooks explains that there was a period when he and his mother were not on speaking terms because she believed she deserved more money than he was allocating. "I had not reneged on giving her x-amount of dollars," he says. "I honored what I promised, so she needed to honor her promise by saving more money."[3] The amount of money he was allocating to his mother was based on his desire to continue to provide for her even after his retirement. That would not be possible if he were allocating the amount she believed was appropriate.

She was unaware of the big picture concerning taxes, fees, and other line items that cut significantly into her son's earnings. Open and honest communication allowed her to realize that his take-home pay wasn't what she had assumed it to be.

There are many assumptions about how much money athletes actually take home. Yes, many contracts pay significant income. However, after agent commissions and taxes, the take-home pay is a lot less than what the media portrays. You still may not sympathize with the NFL player that receives a $3-million paycheck and ends up taking home just over half that sum after federal taxes, state taxes (depending on residency), FICA, Medicare taxes, and agent fees. The point is that your family needs to understand your plan, savings goals, and responsibilities in order for you to avoid misunderstandings and false expectations regarding your actual financial situation.

It is vital that your plan, like Brooks's plan, is structured based on your needs, not the needs of your family members. Communicate to your family your desire to help them, but also convey your personal financial goals and how your contributions affect your long-term goals.

As a child growing up in Illinois, Eric Steinbach was aware that his parents made financial sacrifices in order to send him and his siblings to Catholic school. When the offensive guard graduated from the University of Iowa in 2003 and was drafted by the Cincinnati Bengals, he decided to repay his parents for some of those sacrifices.

Some athletes assist parents with a specific purchase— Brooks bought his parents a new car—or they give them a prearranged amount of money each month. Others provide assistance through job opportunities. You may decide to appoint your sister to head your private foundation, for example, or hire your best friend to work at a new business you start. I will discuss the value of these options in later chapters.

One plan I have seen athletes use successfully is giving family members prepaid debit cards. The benefit is that a monthly statement is provided with details of where, when, and how much the family members spent. This information shows whether the family members are using the money for intended purposes, so it allows you to make sure the financial help you provide is productive and respected. If the family member is spending the money on pricey jewelry and luxury vacations rather than using it to pay down debts or to fund living expenses, you and your advisors will have the means to reevaluate the arrangement and hold family members accountable.

As an athlete, you must assert yourself in these relationships, not by coming across as a dictator, but as someone in control of the situation. When you have millions of dollars in your pocket, people can easily take advantage of you if you fail to establish boundaries in your personal relationships. But when you're in your late teens or early twenties, establishing boundaries with your family is hardly an easy task. In many instances, an athlete must assert himself as the primary decision maker concerning issues related to his career, taking that responsibility out of the hands of his family.

Regardless of the system you implement, be mindful of the fact that family members are not *entitled* to your money, though they may act as if they believe otherwise. Assert yourself as the key decision maker and let family members know you're in control. Then they can't take advantage of you. This role reversal may be hard, and for many people, it occurs later in life. However, most athletes are forced to deal with this situation earlier due to the circumstances.

Steinbach's agent, Jack Bechta, warned him about the risks of opening his wallet to his family, saying, "If you're a crutch now for your family, you'll always be a crutch."[4] With that in mind, Steinbach has been somewhat stern in controlling how his money is distributed, and his parents and siblings have respected his decisions.

By now, you may be wondering why I'm lingering on this topic. It's simply because money can bring out the worst in people, and you need to be prepared if that happens in your family. I've seen it happen, and the extent to which it occurs in the world of professional sports is in a class all its own. Rather than being grateful for the generosity bestowed upon them, sometimes family members begin to see the athlete in the family as an ATM and act as though they are entitled to a portion of his earnings.

Some of my clients have arranged to deposit a predetermined amount of money in their parents' bank accounts on a routine basis. Most parents are grateful for what truly is a gift, but I've overheard arguments about money between athletes and their parents—the deposit wasn't made on time, for example. Can you imagine what that sort of screaming match could do to you if it happened the night before a game when you need to focus on your performance and mentally prepare for competition? That type of argument does nothing but provide an unnecessary distraction.

So what can you do? The problem is compounded if the athlete gives in to his parents' demands and makes a deposit into their bank account the next morning. He sets a dangerous precedent, showing that others can take control of the situation through manipulation. It would be much better to refuse to let family members stir those types of emotions.

Better yet, sit down and engage your family members in a candid discussion about money and each others' expectations before they try to start that argument. Listen to their expectations, but also impress upon them that they cannot call and ask for money during the season unless it's an emergency. If it *is* an emergency, it is imperative to involve your advisors, too, so they can help you sort through the financial, tax, and legal implications. This will help remove the emotional side of the situation and allow you to focus on your job.

You may ask why your advisors need to be involved. How could there be legal, tax, or financial issues? A real-life example will help you understand the answer. Last fall, a client called and mentioned that he wanted to pay off his parents' $200,000 home mortgage to help relieve some financial burdens. Most athletes simply write a check to the lender or their parents to pay off the mortgage. However, a knowledgeable athlete will first call his attorney or CPA. Why? Because there are tax and legal issues involved in this type of transaction.

First, the $200,000 check was subject to gift tax in 2008 of 45 percent unless my client elected to use his lifetime gift exemption of $1 million.[5] I didn't recommend using his lifetime exemption because that $1 million needed to be preserved for estate planning purposes. Instead, I advised my client to structure a loan to his parents for $200,000 with deferred repayment terms, which he could forgive over time or collect in small pieces, in order to avoid the tax. This simple advice saved my client tens of thousands of dollars in gift tax.

If you find yourself in a similar situation, you need to consult with a CPA and have an attorney draft the note. Once the deal has been handled by the CPA and the attorney, an investment advisor can designate the account from which the funds will be withdrawn to preserve the integrity of your investments.

My clients understand that, sometimes, part of my job is to come across as the bad guy. I sit in living rooms and engage athletes' parents in conversations about how money will be appropriated. That doesn't bother me. It doesn't matter that the message is coming from me, so long as it is being communicated.

In laying a set of ground rules, keep in mind that your lifestyle should mirror your message of financial responsibility. It may be difficult for your family members to respect your ground rules if you're driving a Lamborghini, living in a fifteen-thousand-square-foot house, and partying in swanky clubs five nights a week. If you lead by example, they will be more likely to respect your financial decisions, and you will lessen any strain caused by sudden wealth.

The above ideas are always a work in process. In the beginning, don't expect to figure out every single detail. Financial success can serve to help your family in ways no one would ever expect. There is nothing better than having the resources to financially take care of your family in a responsible manner. Having a thoughtful financial plan that is communicated properly to your family will help avoid conflict while allowing you to celebrate and share your financial success with family members in a constructive way.

Rule 2: Beware of the long-lost cousin.

Athletes on the verge of professional success must also face the reality that ex-girlfriends, estranged parents, long-lost cousins, childhood friends, and countless other people from the past will often come out of the woodwork.

Often these individuals acknowledge past misdeeds that may have impacted the relationship. They claim repentance and ask to be welcomed back into the athlete's life. I believe in forgiveness. I believe in redemption. My main concern is whether that repentance is genuine because, in most cases, it is motivated by money. You have to ask, "Would this person be back in my life if I were working for minimum wage?" The problem is, you just don't know. You may forgive an old friend who later reverts back to his old ways.

It is imperative to plan for those situations before becoming successful and wealthy. Again, approaching those situations requires a level of assertiveness that may be difficult for the athlete to convey. But he must effectively communicate the boundaries of the relationship or run the risk of having that person become a thorn in his side and a constant source of stress. Once they are back in my clients' lives, many people ask for money, and my clients often find it hard to say no. One of my clients came to me because he was troubled by a former high school coach's request for a $500,000 loan. He knew granting a loan of that size would be a risky move. But he also struggled with the thought of turning his back on his coach, a man he credited for his success at the professional level.

Athletes must be prepared to face these situations, however difficult they might be. That doesn't mean turning down every request for money that comes at you. It means empowering yourself to be assertive and establish parameters in those relationships.

Retired NFL offensive tackle Tony Boselli approaches all of these requests similarly, recalling advice he received early in his career: "Don't lend money ever unless you plan on just giving it away." If an immediate family member is in need of financial help, it's a no-brainer, according to Boselli. "You help your family," he says. Outside that immediate circle, he recommends that you seek professional guidance. "If it's a distant relative, unless you really feel like they're in dire straits or something terrible is going to happen, my suggestion would be to approach it like any other business deal," Boselli says. "Get advice. And if it doesn't make financial sense, I would not do it."[6]

Whether you are approached by a long-lost cousin or a sibling, do not get in the habit of financially supporting everyone who comes to you for help. Unfortunately, some family and friends will only surface in order to take advantage of your wealth. Make sure to involve your advisors, and don't be afraid to assert yourself and communicate boundaries. If those family and friends don't respect or honor your boundaries, then you need to evaluate whether they have your best interests in mind.

Rule 3: Don't let fame change you.

Wealth and fame come hand in hand in the world of professional sports, and both are intoxicating. You eat at nice restaurants, socialize with beautiful people, fly in private jets, and party at exclusive clubs where everyone is nice to you.

People can become consumed by that lifestyle. I've seen it at the highest level. Sure, it's fun and exciting. But it's also superficial and can cause you to lose sight of your priorities as a professional, as a family member, and as a friend. Professional athletes must be conscious of the pros and cons of that lifestyle, and then decide, based on their own priorities and values, whether they are going to embrace that lifestyle, ignore it, or learn how to balance it.

As an athlete faced with this alluring lifestyle, you must be aware of the fact that, long after you're done playing at the professional level, that lifestyle will still be there for someone else to enjoy.

There is nothing wrong with enjoying the good life. But the minute you allow that lifestyle to negatively impact your decisions (you start to make spontaneous financial decisions, for example) or your relationships (you're not being honest and forthright with the people you love), that is the minute you must reevaluate how you're managing success.

I know many people who, in the process of becoming successful professional athletes, have become celebrities and, in the process, have lost touch with the true substance of their being. As an advisor, it's hard for me to help those clients realize their long-term goals because their decisions can become too impulsive and self-centered, rather than rational or responsible.

The celebrity lifestyle can produce a snowball effect that starts with a modest home, which grows to a five-thousand-square-foot home, which becomes twelve thousand square feet and then twenty-five thousand. It's not that successful athletes don't deserve nice things, but financial projections and long-term savings goals will illustrate that some of them simply can't afford a twelve-thousand-square-foot house. On occasion, some can afford a home that size. However, this decision is often driven by social pressure or unrealistic earning assumptions and not based on what the client really wants or feels comfortable with.

Avoiding the lure of the celebrity lifestyle also means surrounding yourself with people who see the world in a similar light. The danger lies in associating with friends and advisors who are caught up in the mirage of the celebrity lifestyle. Only then does it become difficult to discern what is real and what is superficial. There are accounts of athletes who began to enjoy the celebrity aspect more than playing sports. This is typically the case when an athlete's appearances at nightclubs or celebrity functions drive his schedule and priorities. On occasion, the athlete's friends and associates become part of that lifestyle, and from that point, the risk of drug and alcohol abuse increases, as well as the risk of violence and unhealthy relationships.

Enjoy the ride, enjoy your financial success, but remain balanced and in control of your spending habits and values. Make sure to understand your financial plan before you decide to splurge or invest in expensive assets. Talk to your CPA, attorney, and financial advisor. Most importantly, don't let fame or celebrity status drive you, and don't forget where you came from or who you were before your financial success.

Rule 4: Don't mix business with family.

I have frequently run into situations in which an athlete has hired a family member to manage his insurance, investments, tax planning, or other business interests. That is, perhaps, the biggest mistake an athlete can make. Many don't think twice about it, particularly if a family member is trained and experienced in that area. Perhaps your brother is a CPA, or your aunt is a lawyer. You may think you're an exception to the rule. You're not. It's still a bad idea.

Though it is acceptable to seek the advice of family members on these issues, it becomes dangerous when the family member crosses the line and becomes a paid advisor or gatekeeper as it relates to your financial, tax, or legal issues and business dealings.

Though there will always be exceptions to this, I never recommend it. When you begin to assign critical, substantive tasks to family members, it immediately creates conflict. If their performance is below average, how can you tell them? Could you fire them? Given that money is a difficult subject to breach with family members, how will you negotiate their salary, wages, or fees? Who will verify the accuracy of their work? Who will ensure they are always looking out for your best interests?

If you find yourself at odds or in disagreement with an independent, third-party advisor, you can step away from the situation, reevaluate the relationship, and determine the best course of action. If that advisor is your father, a conflict tied to your professional interests may drive a wedge into your personal relationship, leaving the issue unresolved. You may approach the situation by trying to empower him to be a better advisor, and he may see it as you trying to empower him to be a better father.

A possible alternative is to hire a family member to be your manager, serving as more of a personal consultant than a paid advisor. I consider that to be the least of all evils because a consultant is not responsible for any substantive function such as tax preparation, legal services, or investment management. A personal consultant simply helps you deal with your various advisors when you are busy during your playing season. Though they will not be in a position to provide advice critical to your long-term financial goals or tax planning, they will still expect to be paid for their work. This option is still risky because the consultants may think they are smarter than the advisors in areas they really know nothing about, or they may exert power or influence over your advisors that you have not allowed.

Situations such as these create undue stress for the athlete. But in many situations, the family member suffers as well.

Moms and dads, brothers and sisters, and aunts and uncles have come to me to vent their frustrations over tasks that were assigned to them that are beyond their capabilities.

It's best to hire nonfamily members as your key advisors. Family can be instrumental in helping identify advisors, managing advisors, or providing info to guide your advisors' recommendations. Outside of these areas, by hiring nonfamily members, you will minimize conflicts of interest and ensure accountability for the services delivered.

Rule 5: Make time for family.

As an athlete, you are not unlike other working professionals—you're busy. Think of all that time in the gym and time spent on practice or traveling to games. You communicate with advisors, get involved in communities, do media interviews, and make public appearances. You may even run a business. Your seasons are crazy, and it's just as crazy in the off-season when you handle business matters or travel. Suddenly, you are so busy that you have forgotten to do the little things that make a difference in the lives of your family members. For example, you may forget to call your mother, send a card to your brother on his birthday, or visit your grandparents. Even if your omission is as small as not making a phone call or writing a letter, your failure to recognize the importance of simple things can lead to fractured relationships. The little things should not become burdensome obligations. But if you're too busy to call your sister, you're not managing your time appropriately.

Your family understands that you might not visit as often and that your phone calls might not be as frequent. That comes with growing up and starting a life of your own. But don't drop off the face of the earth. No matter how busy you may be, there's never an excuse for putting your family second to your career.

You may think you have reasons for putting off your family, perhaps because of an ugly past. Though it may seem like a valid excuse, it is all the more reason to reevaluate the relationship and find a way to deal with any hard feelings in a constructive way, rather than choosing to forget someone exists. Despite financial and athletic success, your journey may be much more rewarding with your family members, no matter how imperfect, beside you. Sharing athletic success with your loved ones can enrich the experience and provide support for you during times when things are not going as well. My clients reconnect with certain family members at different stages of their lives, but they always seem happier once they reconnect.

Maintaining a balance between your personal and professional lives will not only please your family, it will make you a happier person. It is possible to be in demand and still be the same son or daughter, brother or sister that you've always been. It requires critical time management, but that balance is good for your soul.

Furthermore, maintaining a successful balance serves as an example to friends and family that you can be a successful athlete with endorsement deals and a handful of charitable commitments and still make time for family. By seeing you make that effort, they will be empowered to do the same.

Rule 6: Empower by example.

I stress to my clients that financial success achieved through athletics is a blessing that presents an opportunity for self-discovery. Some choose to simply go through the motions of their lives and careers. But for others, that journey is overwhelmingly positive and transformational, not only for the athletes but for their families as well. Through leadership, self-improvement, and charitable giving, you can show your family members a side of the world they might not have otherwise known.

There is a sense of empowerment that comes along with having a successful, professional athlete in the family. But empowerment means nothing if family members fail to use it. They have the ability to translate professional success into something bigger than the athlete's on-the-field achievements, bigger than football or basketball, bigger than a multimillion-dollar salary and endorsement contracts. With success comes social responsibility. An athlete's entire family is suddenly in a position to change unhealthy lifestyles and redirect their energies toward something more constructive.

If your transition from amateur to professional athletics is managed appropriately, you will have the ability to make a difference financially in the lives of family members spanning multiple generations. Family members may never again have to work and instead can donate their time to charitable organizations. They may never have to borrow money for school, or be forced to work at a job they don't enjoy. I have clients who are single-handedly responsible for their parents and siblings no longer working minimum wage. They left low-paying jobs to return to school, graduate, and secure better opportunities. That is all because of the genesis of one person.

I believe most human beings struggle through life to become better people. We give of our time and money to see that we leave the world a better place than we found it. For a professional athlete, that very personal journey takes place under a sharp lens.

Those efforts often become an amazingly powerful beacon. Some of my clients truly inspire me and make me realize I need to do more with my life. Athletes, simply through the example they set on and off the field, can empower their family members and others to improve their own lives and personal situations.

Most people look back on their lives wishing they had done more with their time and money. Don't go through life regretting what you could have done. Rather, be able to look at yourself in the mirror and say, "I made the most of that journey."

Chapter 2

Consider the Value of Spirituality

When I first began working as an advisor to professional athletes, one common thread among many of my clients was their spirituality. Though not all subscribed to the beliefs of a specific religion, they put their faith in a higher power and made the conscious decision to live their lives in accordance with those beliefs.

Athletes with a sincere commitment to spiritual enrichment, whether expressed outwardly or observed privately, typically feel they are able to better endure many of the challenges that await them during the difficult transition from amateur to professional sports, constant public criticism, unhealthy temptations, and reentry into the "real world." From the many discussions I've had with athletes, I can see that they often lean on their spirituality to guide them and help them overcome adversity in the many risks and challenges that confront them as a result of their profession.

Professional athletics places men and women in situations in which family, friends, fans, and countless others are continually trying to position themselves to take advantage of not only their personal fame and fortune, but also access to opportunities. Spirituality often can help enable an athlete to manage that journey in a way that allows them to maintain a sense of self and continue on a path of personal growth. Empathy and belief in something larger than yourself may help you identify and connect with others who are less fortunate and provide them with inspiration and guidance.

"I think (faith) needs to be the number one priority in (an athlete's) life as a human being," Derrick Brooks says.[1] He feels an athlete must align his priorities, with faith being number one, followed by family, and then career. By keeping those priorities in order, Brooks says, athletes will be better equipped to handle life's challenges. In my own experience, I've found this to be true. When you come into money and fame, certain people will disappoint you if you don't provide for them financially, and there will always be a certain group of people who are looking for you to fail. When you are able to put certain challenges in perspective and deal with them in a constructive manner, you feel more in control when facing these challenges.

Athletes who enter the professional arena grounded in spirituality have an experience that often lies in contrast with that of their peers. Their positive demeanor and healthy outlook on life allow them to maintain a balanced family life and healthy relationships with their loved ones, friends, organization, teammates, advisors, and the league.

"We are physical beings, emotional beings, and spiritual beings," Tony Boselli says. "Since I'm a Christian, I think faith in Jesus is paramount to a good foundation and is a baseline for making life's choices—everything from marriage and raising kids and business decisions to what kind of character you demonstrate and how you live your life."[2]

Regardless of your specific spiritual beliefs, it is critical to understand the value of a balanced spiritual perspective on success and fame as it relates to making the most of an athlete's opportunity on and off the field. The rules provided below will help athletes integrate their spirituality during their professional career in an effort to achieve and protect their spiritual identity.

Rule 1: Use your professional journey as an opportunity to explore your spirituality.

An athlete's journey through his career in professional sports is transformational on many levels. Spiritual self-discovery is not exempt and, in fact, is often at the center of that transformation. If an athlete begins his professional career unattached to a particular faith or religion, he often finds himself drawn to one at some point during his playing years.

Boselli was raised by parents who taught him how to live life according to the Catholic faith. "But I was like most teenagers and college kids and knew better than everybody else and lived life how I wanted to for quite a while," he says.[3] After his first year in the NFL, he was reintroduced to the Christian faith and made the decision to follow Jesus and live his life accordingly.

Boselli's experience is not unlike that of many other current and former pro athletes. Few twenty-one-year-olds enter the pro draft deeply rooted in faith, even if they attended weekly religious services throughout their childhood. They are only beginning to discover their faith.

However, in some cases, adversity forced religious and spiritual maturity on athletes at a young age. Some of my clients grew up in single-parent households or broken homes, or were raised by a grandparent or older sibling. Others come from hardworking families that struggled through financial issues, health problems, and in many cases, the influences of drugs and crime. Others were dealt a traumatic blow through an event such as the death of a parent or loved one.

When a young person is faced with difficult circumstances, athletics can be an escape, as can spirituality. Certain young men and women in these situations tend to embrace spirituality and, in contrast with their peers, become more versed in its applicability to their daily lives. They seek out something that will provide support as they face tough decisions and temptations.

While a student at Florida State University, Brooks's main vice was alcohol. He even admits to downing a beer before heading across campus to take an exam. "I felt that was just part of who I was," he says. That is, until a friend, whose father was in poor health, quit drinking as he prayed for his recovery. He realized he had always asked God for favors but never gave up anything for God. Brooks acknowledged what he believed to be a noble act by his friend, but responded by simply saying, "Well, that's more for me." That conversation stuck with Brooks, though, and finally he realized that, if he wanted to seek out a more personal relationship with God, he needed to give up drinking. "I think by making that decision, that kind of started filling in the cracks in my foundation. It allowed me to stand up and start being a man."[4]

Rule 2: Spirituality can be a guide through the ups and downs of your career.

Spirituality provides balance and stability in the chaotic and busy world that surrounds professional athletes. It can ground them during a high-stress, high-pressure career and provide direction when they are faced with a preponderance of negative influences, all of which can lure athletes away from their efforts to achieve personal happiness and professional success.

Spirituality is about more than subscribing to or memorizing certain teachings or doctrines. It is about applying those teachings in your daily life. Tiger Woods subscribes to Buddhist teachings and was quoted in *Sports Illustrated* explaining that Buddhism involves a kind of macrodiscipline and that the structure of your life has to serve the larger purpose of perfecting your game. "I like Buddhism because it's a whole way of being and living," Woods said. "It's based on discipline and respect and personal responsibility."[5]

On the other hand, Tim Tebow, quarterback for the University of Florida, inked "John 3:16" into his eye black before the BCS Championship game in 2009. Tebow has dedicated most of his life to helping others, caring for the impoverished, and applying his faith in his daily life. University of Florida head coach Urban Meyers said in a telephone interview with the *New York Times*, "His whole purpose of playing football and being Tim Tebow is to use it as a platform to spread his faith."[6]

On the field performance, contracts, endorsements, signing bonuses, and the social scene—to name a few things—make the pro sports world undeniably self-absorbed. Spirituality allows you to take a look at life's challenges from an alternative viewpoint. When you stop to think, meditate, or pray, you are able to take a step back from a situation, however big or small it may be, and see how it affects you and those around you. For an athlete, such perspective can create clarity, perspective, and empathy.

Spirituality can provide a sense of balance, allowing you to see that there is more to life than your internal battles, such as struggling to perform at a level that meets coaches' expectations or dealing with contract negotiations that don't go your way. When an athlete can take that thread of spirituality and weave it into the other pieces of his or her journey—charitable giving, for example—the athlete's focus shifts from self to others.

An athlete's spiritual side also allows him to see there is more to life than the ups and downs of his career. A year-long cycle—preseason, season, and off-season—can be an emotional roller coaster. During the preseason, my clients are consumed with getting back in shape—after a few months off—and preparing themselves mentally and physically for preseason practices. During the season, days and weeks are filled with interviews, meetings, public appearances, family obligations, and countless other responsibilities that add to the pressure of regular practices, preparation, games, and frequent travel. Suddenly, the season comes to an abrupt end. For some players, that letdown affects them in a way that alters their mood for weeks, sometimes months, primarily because they find themselves at home with little to occupy their time.

Unless an urgent matter arises, I usually give my clients a couple weeks after their season ends to decompress. Otherwise, during this period, I struggle to keep some of them on course with their affairs because they are not sure what to do with their free time and typically need time to settle back into a routine. During that off-season funk, it is important that athletes look at their situation with some degree of levity. I have observed that athletes with some degree of spiritual focus are able to celebrate life outside the context of a victory and away from the excitement of the season. Their mood for the first four months of the off-season isn't determined by whether the season ended on a good or bad note. They tend to be more settled in who they are as a person outside of athletics.

Typically, following a bad season, an athlete is faced with many questions, including job security, the opportunity to play in the future for his or her current team, health issues, and, most importantly, the psychology of gearing up for another season when the chances of success seem unlikely or unclear. Clear spiritual guidance helps athletes address such issues by helping them realize they can only control certain aspects of the future—the rest is up to a higher power. This view can serve to relieve some of the stress and uncertainty associated with a career in professional sports.

I am by no means stating that certain professional athletes with some level of sincere spirituality are more successful on the playing field. However, one of my jobs as an advisor to my clients is to prepare them as spouses, parents, friends, business partners, or leaders to become well-rounded and personally satisfied with their on- and off-the-field accomplishments long after their playing career is over.

Brooks finds it hard to attribute his success on the football field to his faith in God. "It's like saying God plays favorites," Brooks says. Nor does he believe he can use his faith as a bargaining chip when it comes to his career. "It's not like I'm going to read the Bible five times a day now and that will get four more wins. You read the Bible five times a day to be a better person, and hopefully by being a better person, you'll be a better person for your team, and your team will be successful because it's a better team."[7]

Boselli had already experienced a great deal of success before turning his life over to God, having been the number two overall pick of the 1995 NFL draft. He lived on the edge during his first year in the league and points to current and former pro athletes who live hard and are enormously successful.

"That catches up with you sooner or later," Boselli says. "You're playing Russian roulette, and sooner or later you're going to get caught off the field in a compromising situation, or in a situation where you break the law and you get in trouble. You're going to get in trouble with the league, and you're going to get in trouble with your community, which then ends up hurting your club. It hurts your family, it hurts you, and it hurts your future earning power, because now you have this stigma of being the guy who got in trouble off the field. And that hurts marketing, business opportunities, everything else. The choices we make have a great effect on our lives in the future." Boselli believes faith spared him from the dangers presented by that lifestyle and realizes that, had he continued to live life the way he had, it could have threatened his career. He says his newfound spiritual journey changed his foundation and how he lives his life, and it affects the choices he makes on a daily basis. "What you do off the field always affects your career and how you play. In that sense, it has a huge impact on it."[8]

Rule 3: Be sincere.

Professional athletes who describe themselves as spiritual have to make the conscious decision as to whether they should present their spiritual side as part of their public image. Some are very open with their faith, hoping to provide spiritual inspiration, while others prefer to keep their faith private.

Unfortunately, some players see faith and spirituality as tools to be used for personal gain or opportunity or to mask otherwise less desirable lifestyle choices. However, any lack of sincerity as it relates to your spirituality is so transparent that it is futile to even try to put on a false front. It causes more harm than good, costing you the respect of your coaches, teammates, and fans, most of whom would prefer you to show your true self.

It has played out thousands of times before: An athlete sits down for a postgame press conference and proceeds to "thank God" for allowing him to sink a last-second three-pointer or for sending a game-winning home run over the left field wall. Most athletes who offer thanks to God are sincere. However, some live their lives in ways that fail to reflect what they preach.

As an athlete, you may think such "spiritually inspired" statements are perfect for a sound byte on ESPN and will provide a boost to your public image. They might be. But people who really know you and see you as more than a commodity can sniff out insincere intentions. Eric Steinbach points to numerous players he has met during his first four years in the NFL who carry their Bibles around the locker room but who live their lives in contrast to what they preach—partying hard, cheating on spouses, deceiving friends and family, and living on the edge.[9]

Spirituality can be a very personal and intimate experience for many of us.

As a result, I do not pass judgment on anyone as it relates to their faith. Whether a client's faith is rooted in Christian, Buddhist, or Jewish beliefs is not important to me as an advisor. Some of my clients are still exploring, questioning, and challenging their faith and commitment to various organized religions. Some of my clients don't practice any form of spirituality whatsoever. Some are so dedicated to their faith that every substantive decision in their life is a reflection of their spiritual base. Regardless of your faith or lack thereof, it is imperative that you're honest with yourself and others as to where you stand. Such honesty will endure through your relationships even as your spiritual journey unfolds throughout life's many twists and turns.

Rule 4: Buck the pressure to be perfect.

Professional athletes put an incomparable amount of time, energy, and dedication into achieving perfection, whether that's diet and exercise, on-the-field performance, or knowledge of their sport, for example. They put pressure on themselves to be perfect and face pressure from fans and the media to perform error-free through the last second of each game. It's in an athlete's blood and in their nature to try to achieve perfection. From the time an athlete steps foot on the playing field as a young child, competition and pride play a critical role in the pursuit of perfection and winning. At the same time, when you achieve a level of financial and personal success as a professional athlete, fear of losing that success often drives your passion and pursuit of perfection on the field.

But the reality is that nobody will ever be perfect at anything forever and success at the highest levels is fleeting. Understanding one's spirituality allows that person to achieve a deeper understanding of his purpose in life. Your career is a part of you; it doesn't define you. It enables an athlete to step back and say to himself, "I may not be the fastest player on my team or have an optimal body fat percentage for my position, but that's okay because I'm providing my team with something else of value." It's okay if you're not a standout rebounder because you're the best three-point shooter in the league, or that you're not perfect at pass coverage because you're a phenomenal tackler.

Of course, you want to excel at all aspects of your game, as do your coaches and teammates. That pressure can build to a point at which you take the sport too seriously and are unable to perform up to the level of expectation you set for yourself—and then you become paralyzed.

Accepting your downfalls and embracing your strengths eliminates a major burden. It allows a player to accept the undeniable truth: You do not have to be perfect in all aspects of your profession in order to be successful on or off the field. Once you come to terms with your limitations and focus on your strengths, you can truly soar. I have always believed you should work and focus on your strengths and acknowledge your weaknesses. If you have a cannon for an arm, but no agility or quickness, work on your pocket passing and reading coverage. It is more likely you will come closer to achieving a high level of success as a pocket passer than as a scrambling, freestyle, elusive passer. Obviously, this analogy applies to any position, sport, or career.

Rule 5: Spirituality does not inhibit competitiveness.

My clients who place faith and spirituality at the top of their priority list express a deep respect for others. At the same time, they step onto the field or court every game with the intention of either physically beating their opponents or winning the game through high-level physical performance. Though some may object, those players make it quite obvious that you can be a fierce competitor and still be considered faithful, spiritual, or religious.

Brutal physical contact is a part of certain sports. Athletes—football players in particular—step onto the field with a kill-or-be-killed mentality and accept the risks associated with physical play.

A spiritually guided athlete should not be led to believe that their competitiveness compromises their personal morals or values. It is possible to separate the man who steps out onto the baseball diamond to compete from the man who goes home to his family at night, attends weekly religious services, and volunteers in his community.

My clients who consider themselves religious or spiritual have a sense of self that enables them to harness their intense competitiveness and to turn it on and off at the appropriate times. Spirituality does not cloud their competitive spirit. It is not a sign of weakness, and as a player you should never be led to believe that being spiritual means you have to soften up. Rather, develop an understanding of how to separate the two personas.

Rule 6: Embrace your obligations as a role model.

When you enter a situation in which you are collecting a sizable salary and have earned the status of a successful athlete, I have always believed you have an obligation to positively influence others.

That obligation does not require you to spend every available moment working to change the world. It should, however, influence the way you conduct yourself on and off the field and the way you treat your teammates, coaches, media, fans, members of the community, and family members.

In my experiences, I have found that athletes who have some spiritual base tend to be more supportive of being a role model and understand the positive effect that role models can have on young children and others. Their focus is on living life in accordance with their personal set of morals and values, often influenced by their faith. They understand how their actions and attitudes can influence young people who look up to them, and they are mindful of the watchful eyes of those youngsters who are quick to mimic those they admire.

An athlete's faith can also, in itself, serve to influence young minds. Young people often find it hard to believe that you can be cool, talented, athletic, competitive, and aggressive and still take time out to be thankful. Proving otherwise by example sends a powerful message.

Being a spiritual role model does not entail preaching from the Bible or teaching Sunday school classes. When spirituality plays a role in your daily life and you're open about it, it is inspiring.

Your message is particularly relevant at a time when children are struggling to discover their own identity and path in life. Your athletic abilities make you a role model in the eyes of many children, and your message of faith and spirituality will likely resonate deeper than it would if it were coming from a parent or teacher.

Rule 7: Hire advisors who respect your spirituality or lack thereof.

In hiring advisors, it is imperative that you evaluate their professional qualifications while also taking into consideration your connection with them on a more personal level. That does not mean, however, that you should select advisors based on their faith. That is a mistake. One of my clients made this mistake, and it cost him dearly. He was approached by a fellow Bible study group member who sold financial products, so he bought a financial product from his friend without having his advisors review the proposal. After spending hundreds of thousands of dollars and losing most of the money he had invested in the financial product, my client realized that he had purchased the wrong type of product. His mistake could have sent him into bankruptcy without his attorney's intervention.

Find an advisor who will serve you and help you achieve your goals, one who won't cloud the relationship with their religious convictions or yours. A mutual respect between client and advisor is very important. As an athlete, you know the type of person with whom you want to do business. Stick to those guidelines.

Chapter 3

Build a Winning Team of Advisors

Young athletes preparing for the transition from amateur to professional level are faced with the prospect of earning significant income. In addition, they may receive a signing bonus that will dwarf the annual salary of their college classmates, not to mention the potential for a multimillion-dollar endorsement income that will follow.

In order to deal with all the issues that go along with significant wealth, one must hire certain financial, tax, and legal advisors. The advisor selection process is very important and often a misunderstood process. It is not just about selecting a contract agent. It also involves selecting a tax team, legal team, business consulting team, marketing team, and investment team—just to name a few. Questions such as whether all of these services should be offered by an agent, an agent's office, or independent firms are critical for athletes and their families to analyze. Most professional athletes fail to prepare for these issues prior to receiving their first paycheck and do not assemble their team, outside of an agent and maybe an investment advisor, in advance.

Some athletes receive their first paycheck and are uncertain as to where it should be deposited, how much should be saved, spent, invested, how the account should be titled, etc. Tampa Bay's Derrick Brooks put his first check in a money market account and left it untouched for one year. He said he was driven by fear that his playing years would be short-lived and his money would disappear. "I did nothing until I understood what all this money was," he says.[1]

That fear and uncertainty, which festers in the minds of many young athletes at the start of their careers, is evidence as to why the central focus of a player's journey should be assembling a team of qualified and reliable advisors to aid the athlete throughout their careers and well into retirement. But it is essential that you engage those advisors before the transition gains steam to ensure you have a solid understanding of what you can expect to see when you start making money.

"What athletes don't realize is the moment they sign for all this money, they become a business, they become a corporation, they are an entity with tax issues, with business issues, with exposure, with opportunity, with all sorts of things," Tony Boselli says. "And they need to hire a consultant or somebody who is in their corner who is an expert at that."[2]

But many of these athletes, aligned with some of the best agents in the business, fail to recognize the value of an advisory team, a team that should include—in addition to their agent—a financial advisor, an attorney, and a qualified accountant or tax advisor at the very least. These separate advisors are the pillars of a transition that will produce long-term success, and they will be the backbone of everything you do during and after your career. The following rules will help you select and identify these advisors in addition to making sure you have a system to measure their performance and value.

Rule 1: Agents are not advisors, and advisors are not agents.

Agents have long been integral players in professional sports, representing athletes at the negotiating table and securing multimillion-dollar contracts, signing bonuses, and endorsement deals. Selecting the right agent at the start of your career is paramount.

But athletes often falter in mistakenly assuming a contract agent is the same as their business, tax, financial, or legal advisor. Assuming they are all one and the same can be a costly mistake, drawing an athlete into a relationship with an agent who is not qualified, licensed, or experienced in offering other services.

There are numerous differentiators that separate agents from advisors, one of the most significant being the duration of the professional relationship. For most players, agents serve a short-term function, negotiating salary contracts with the team and securing endorsement deals and collecting a commission based on a percentage of those earnings. When an athlete retires and is no longer on a team payroll, the agent will no longer earn a percentage of the athlete's contract as compensation. In addition, most endorsements stop at that point. As a result, the agent's services will become less relevant or perhaps nonexistent.

Typically, your tax, legal, financial, and business advisors will be involved long after your professional career in sports is over, assuming your wealth and business interests are sustained and you are pursuing a successful career. Advisors work with clients on business deals, tax matters, and estate planning strategies long after their playing days have ended, perhaps on an even greater scale than while they are playing. Upon their retirement, many athletes have accumulated a sizable net worth and, with more time on their hands, are operating several businesses.

However, many athletes fail to recognize the value of a diversified advisory team while they are in college, entering the draft, or in their first few years in the league. It's difficult to think far ahead, particularly when you are in your early twenties and just launching your career. Following retirement, your life won't be as glamorous and you won't be earning as much income, but you will still want to have an advisor whom you can call and ask for help related to investments, legal and tax issues, planned giving, and business deals.

Some agents represent themselves as a one-stop shop, claiming they can manage a client's contract negotiations as well as his financial, business, legal, and tax affairs. Agents may employ specialists to offer such services as part of their "fee." Some of these employed specialists (CPA, attorney, etc.) are qualified, and others are not. Regardless of qualifications, it is imperative that you hire *independent* advisors that are not a part of your agent's office. Why? By keeping all of your advisory functions with one individual or company, you remove true and perceived accountability among advisors. Therefore, you lack any checks and balances that relate to making sure your advisory team is also accountable to others. If one person serves as your agent, manages your investments, handles your tax planning, brings you business deals, and represents you on legal matters, there is no one who will make sure that person is not promoting or selling services or products that are not suitable for your planning needs.

A legal advisor provides guidance regarding how accounts should be legally titled, the asset protection afforded those accounts, how to preserve assets in light of a lawsuit, estate planning, corporate structure, risk management with partners, prenuptial planning, and countless other legal issues that an athlete may encounter during his career and in retirement. And yet many athletes operate under the false assumption that, because they've never faced criminal charges, they don't need a legal advisor or that their financial advisor can answer these questions. Keep in mind, an investment advisor is not permitted to provide legal or tax advice outside of their specific investment services.

A tax advisor's relevance extends far beyond tax season. A seven-figure salary from your team, coupled with earnings from endorsement contracts and outside business deals, presents complex tax issues that require review and consideration of certain complex tax structures and planning.

Each advisor is one part of the foundation. Each has his own tasks and responsibilities, but the team is not fully functional unless each member is bringing to the table his own expertise. They not only provide a comprehensive approach to wealth planning, but they are part of a system of checks and balances that promotes accountability from all advisors and better serves the athlete's interests.

Brooks says his agent only negotiates his football contract, and he cautions other players about the risks of selecting an agent who stretches into other advisory roles. "A young player generally—because of the fact that young players get overwhelmed early—would tend to trust an agent who says they can do all these services," Brooks says. "But I caution the ones who think that way, because you can't have all your eggs in one basket. Where is your system of checks and balances?"[3]

Rule 2: Understand the value of an advisory team.

Understanding the role and purpose of an advisory team can be difficult for a twenty-year-old to grasp. The relevance of a financial advisor is obvious to many—Derrick Brooks, Tony Boselli, and Eric Steinbach all hired a financial advisor right out of the gate—but it becomes more difficult to explain the importance of hiring an attorney and an accountant independent of the agent as part of a team of advisors.

Countless players have underestimated the need for those key advisors and, in doing so, have been led to trust the wrong people and make quick investment decisions that failed, often because they lacked a sounding board of professionals who could provide advice based on a thorough analysis of a proposal.

Boselli says an athlete must first hire his agent and then, before he collects a paycheck, hire a tax, legal, and financial advisor who will talk him through the financial issues he now faces. Of course, that's a slice out of the athlete's paycheck, and many rookies are hesitant to start cutting into their earnings so quickly. Boselli says it's worth it and money you spend on an advisor is money well spent, saving you serious losses in bad investments down the road. "I think the challenge in trying to deal with these young athletes—and I was one of them—is the lack of education, the lack of understanding about how things work," Boselli says. "The advice I would give young guys is, 'Listen, go get an expert or a professional in the field who handles high net worth individuals' money who aren't athletes. Go find those individuals who might not necessarily work with athletes but deal with high net worth individuals. Engage in a relationship like that because it will be the best thing you ever can do and it will protect you in the long run and save you a ton of money.'"[4]

If you know that your financial, legal, and tax affairs are being managed by competent professionals, you have the time and energy to focus on your sport, your family, and community service commitments, which should be your priorities.

Too often, I meet with a potential client who has selected an agent and, in some cases, a marketing advisor. The last item on their "to do" list is to hire financial, legal, and tax advisors. That approach is counter to how the process should operate, placing emphasis on strike-while-the-iron-is-hot opportunities rather than long-term planning. Furthermore, I warn many clients about the danger of having their agents drive or hire financial, tax, business, and legal advisors. When that happens, there can be an immediate conflict of interest in that most of those advisors don't want to upset the agent since he is the one who is responsible for making them money. In these situations, you won't see too many disagreements among advisors on any issue because no one wants to upset the guy who brought them to the table.

Many athletes, particularly first-round draft picks who will be among the highest-paid rookies, seek out a financial advisor to manage the significant amount of money they will soon collect. A financial advisor is an invaluable member of the advisory team, and selecting a financial advisor whom you can trust with your money is of the utmost importance.

However, you cannot take full advantage of your financial advisor if he operates in a vacuum. Rather, he should be partnered with a team of advisors, giving you a more comprehensive approach to wealth planning. As much as we are talking about financial growth, we're also talking about wealth preservation, which is possible only by incorporating financial planning with legal and tax planning.

Rule 3: Review an advisor's background.

Finding advisors is never an issue for promising youth athletes. They are inundated with phone calls and knocks on the door from advisors seeking out their business. The challenge lies in selecting the *right* advisors—those who are responsible, trustworthy, experienced, and qualified to oversee the unique aspects of an athlete's wealth plan.

One of the critical first steps in the hiring process is to ensure any potential advisor has undergone some form of due diligence. For lawyers, look to certification as a member of their state bar association, which will tell you if the lawyer has ever been disciplined or had his or her license suspended, revoked, or reinstated.

Brokers are regulated by the Financial Industry Regulatory Association (FINRA), which provides public information related to whether an investment broker has personally been subject to regulatory discipline. To find information about investment brokers' firms or individual advisors, you may visit www.finra.org. The Securities Exchange Commission (SEC) provides information and background on investment brokers' firms and advisors at www.adviserinfo.sec.gov. The confusion regarding these separate regulatory bodies, along with how they can best protect investors from fraud, is being reconsidered since the financial meltdown of 2008 and the Madoff scandal. There is a current movement to unify the standard of care and extend the fiduciary obligations of an advisor to brokers. Nevertheless, investors should continue to check both resources for past disciplinary issues related to brokers or the investment firms brokers work for.

CPAs can be researched by checking with the American Institute of Certified Public Accountants (AICPA) online at www.aicpa.org.

In addition to the above, reference checks and criminal background checks will provide you further information. Finally, references from existing clients can be a good source of information to consider as well. Be wary of advisors for whom there are no means to investigate their backgrounds. Beware of credentials for which there is no transparency and of advisors for whom there is no reliable information from a trusted source.

Organizations such as the National Football League Players Association (NFLPA) offer an appointment process for advisors other than contract agents. There is some controversy whether such certification is truly reliable. When I decided to become an advisor to NFL players, I applied to the NFLPA for certification. I went through an extensive application process that took into consideration my education, background, references, criminal record, and credit record. Upon screening all those details, the league granted approval for my certification, an indication to players that I had undergone and passed the NFLPA's due diligence process. However, keep in mind that such certifications will not guarantee that an approved advisor's staff member handling a certain function is qualified or that the approved advisor will always act in good faith. Nevertheless, the NFLPA certification process at least allows the player to know that the advisor's past conduct and qualifications have been investigated and reviewed.

An independent background check is also essential. Who is this person? What does he do away from his job? What is his family situation? What type of person is he away from the office? Looking into an advisor's educational background is important, but whether he attended Harvard or USC says little about his ability to represent you honestly and ethically. Background information, though seemingly insignificant, lends great insight into an advisor's personality, work ethic, and reliability. There are certain temperaments you will want to see reflected in your advisors—depending on the individual athlete—and background information can help guide you to the appropriate candidate.

Athletes should further take advantage of the resources afforded by their teams. In addition to the due diligence process afforded by certain associations, some teams will assist in the process by investigating advisors and their company. A player should feel comfortable asking his team to look into an advisor's credentials on his behalf before agreeing to work with the advisor.

Each athlete should also meet individually with prospective advisors and conduct his or her own evaluations. As an athlete, you need to decide what type of advisor would be best suited to be a part of your advisory team based on your principles, personality, and family situation and make your hiring decisions accordingly.

Eric Steinbach, a graduate of the University of Iowa and member of the Cleveland Browns, received assistance from his alma mater in hiring an agent. Sometimes, coaches screen agents on behalf of the players and at the end of the year select four or five agents for players to interview and hire as they see fit.

"I wanted to be more hands-on," Steinbach says. "So I'd call agents, talk to them on the phone, things like that. When it came down to the last four or five, then I got my family involved for extra advice."[5]

Derrick Brooks assembled a panel that included his parents, a cousin who was also a member of the NFL, and several friends, including a judge. Brooks, who did not sit in on the panel interview, prepared a list of several questions for the group to ask of each candidate. He met with each candidate separately and then compared notes with the group.

He said the diversity of the group made it possible for him to more thoroughly evaluate potential advisors. His parents were able to see qualities in each advisor that he was unable to see on his own. His friend, the judge, provided a thorough evaluation of each individual's character, and his cousin provided valuable insight from a professional athlete's point of view.

"They were a part of the process, but I never let any one of my parents or family friends think they were in control," Brooks says.[6]

Boselli asked his father to sit in on interviews with advisors and now says, "I wish I'd listened to him more. I was twenty-three years old and thought I knew a lot more than I actually did, and he was probably trying to give me more advice than I was listening to." Boselli interviewed three financial advisors and hired one because of his history of working with big-name athletes. Two years later, that financial advisor was convicted of embezzling money and was sentenced to ten years in a federal penitentiary. "That was a rough start," Boselli admits.[7]

Rule 4: Evaluate a potential advisor professionally and personally.

Several factors regarding potential advisors may be evaluated based on your personal preferences. It is better to work with the principals of the company, the owner or a key manager. In certain cases, it is valuable to work with advisors who understand what it means to own and operate a business. Their lessons, experience, and independence can prove to be very valuable as an athlete's career evolves. If you choose to work with an advisor who owns his own business, you must have some information that the business is stable. Your advisor should be hungry for business, but also should be established and successful. There must be enough business coming through the front door to generate long-term stability, which provides you, the client, with a sense of confidence in the long-term viability and service of the company and advisor you are hiring.

A business owner who is suffering financially may make suggestions that are not in your best interest simply because he is strapped for cash and rent is due. When an advisor is stretched too thin, he often pushes clients into transactions, strategies, investments, or products that will generate income for the advisor. Strapped or distressed companies can create a conflict of interest on the part of the advisor and can force the advisor to push services, financial products, or business opportunities that are not suitable for the athlete.

Certain advisors who get behind the eight ball financially will do anything to cover payroll and rent and still be able to collect a salary. But if your advisor has reached a point of professional stability and his or her business is stable financially without insurmountable overhead, the fees or commissions generated from the athlete's business won't make or break next month's payroll. You have to be able to ask an advisor, "If I don't work with you, is your business going to be okay?" The due diligence process will highlight potential problems, as will financial reports from firms that operate as publicly traded companies.

Some degree of trust can be established through the due diligence process, providing assurance that the advisor has a proven track record and is either employed by or operating a stable company. You will continue to build trust in your advisor as your relationship evolves. But at the end of the day, you have to do a gut check and decide whether you can trust this person to a point that you can surrender to him a great deal of control over your financial, tax, business, and/or legal affairs.

This book will help you educate yourself as to the advantages and disadvantages of working with a large brokerage house versus a midlevel boutique firm, which is smaller in size with fewer assets under management. The same method of evaluation applies to the process of selecting a law firm or accounting firm. Consider the value of large versus small, as each has its own pros and cons. Among accounting firms, midsize boutiques tend to be more hands-on than large firms. In the law firm setting, however, your decision should come down to your level of comfort working with a specific attorney from within the firm. Depending on the nature of an athlete's legal needs, in most circumstances, hiring a specific attorney based on his or her experience and skill within a certain area of the law is more important than the name of the firm they are associated with.

Regardless of the size of the firm, you must be assured there is someone within it who will work directly with you to address your needs on a more personal level. You should have a synergy with that person and be on the path toward developing a positive working relationship. That person may not be the firm's leader, but must be someone who can best represent your interests.

Personal relationships and qualifications should drive your decision more than the size of the firm. Whether or not you like an advisor is a consideration that should not be taken lightly, as you'll be working closely with that person for many years to come. If you and your advisor have a personality conflict and lack a basic connection, you need to move on and find another advisor. Life is too short for you to work with somebody with whom you have no interest in talking to. Such a lack of communication will not help to keep your planning needs on task and will disrupt the coordinated effort of your other advisors to handle your needs as well.

Rule 5: Appoint a quarterback.

On countless occasions, a client has come to me with his advisors at his side, and it soon becomes obvious that the right hand doesn't know what the left hand is doing. The financial advisor made a recommendation he never ran by the CPA. The CPA made a counterproposal, but the attorney contends neither position will hold up if challenged. The client becomes the pinball, trying to figure out what is going on because none of his advisors have effectively communicated the details behind the situation.

This illustrates a problem that commonly exists in many of these fragmented advisory situations. There is no single point of entry to the advisory team, which leads to missed phone calls, a lack of follow-through on the part of the advisors, and in the end, an unresolved issue and no one who can be held directly accountable.

If your CPA, attorney, and financial advisor work in separate vacuums and are strictly reactionary, failing to work together to aid their client, it is difficult for any of them to take the initiative and put all the pieces together as they relate to intricate, complex issues. Unless you have someone who can coordinate the advisor's recommendations, your advisors will continue to operate independently without any sense of organization or the overall objective. Accountability is completely absent.

To avoid falling into a fragmented system, your team of advisors must include one individual or firm whom you designate to look at the big picture, which includes tax, legal, marketing, planned giving, and other pieces of the puzzle, and then coordinate that information with separate advisors in a way that sets the course toward achieving specific goals and objectives. It fosters efficiency and accountability and promotes long-term sustained growth.

My company typically serves as the "quarterback" for clients' planning needs by coordinating issues with current advisors, sorting and storing data, and overseeing the risk management needs of athletes. Our clients hire a team of independent advisors representing some or all of those various specialties, with my firm acting as the quarterback to promote collaboration, accountability, and better service to our clients.

This model, sometimes referred to as the "family office" approach, has sparked an ongoing revolution in the industry. For advisors, a family office makes it easier to manage the team at all levels to ensure everyone is working toward the same goal. For an athlete, a family office provides security that an independent team is working on the athlete's behalf to achieve objectives while managing risk.

Unfortunately, advisors may feel threatened by one another. The investment guy doesn't want the insurance guy to sell a product he can sell. The CPA may have an investment division within his office, which threatens the athlete's current investment team. The investment team may offer tax services, and the lawyer may want to handle the taxes. Simply put, a client's best interest will not be served if his advisors feel threatened by one another. On the other hand, a client's best interest will not be served if everyone is too close. For example, a CPA who is brought in by your investment team may not feel comfortable advising against a tax strategy proposed by that same investment team.

My approach to operating a family office is tailored and depends on the professional athlete's circumstances. However, if an athlete is significantly wealthy with a number of business investments, it is necessary to coordinate the decision-making process immediately using independent advisors. If a client's wealth is growing and he or she has yet to invest in significant outside business ventures, we may not formalize a family office quite yet. However, the foundation absolutely needs to be in place to hold quarterly or semiannual meetings with all advisors to ensure the client's matters are being handled with appropriate oversight.

When an athlete sits down at the first "family office" meeting and explains exactly what each advisor's role is and instructs them to cooperate, it is interesting to see the response. You would be amazed how well this model can work when the athlete makes sure the advisors understand that they will be removed from office if they underperform or don't cooperate with one another. If the athlete is passive, unsure, or unable to lead the team of advisors, the athlete is back to the old model, where the risks are higher due to the lack of accountability and independence among advisors. Regardless of whether your team fits under the family office model, you still must appoint a quarterback who does nothing but coordinate and filter information and deal with the minutiae so that, at the end of the day, you're talking to one person instead of four, receiving summaries and specific mandates.

If a quarterback is not there to take the lead, the responsibility falls to the athlete—who does not have the time to deal with the various bits of information coming at him and likely doesn't have the experience, training, or time to understand the intricate details of those areas of expertise to correctly interpret and translate the information. In addition, he lacks the ability to step away from the situation and evaluate the root of the problem. If my client is having a bad week, I can see that and know that I need to spearhead an effort to know the issue hanging over his head and make sure it gets addressed. An athlete who is forced to quarterback his advisory team is unable to take that approach and is constantly bogged down by details of his wealth planning efforts.

Turning over the reins to a quarterback requires an athlete to relinquish some control, which is not always easy. Control is everything. Some clients say, "I don't want to deal with it. You take care of it." Others say, "I don't want to entrust you with all of that." The level of control an athlete is willing to hand off depends on several factors, including the complexity of his situation and his or her nature. Be mindful that turning over the responsibility of your advisory team to a quarterback may be difficult, but it will save you an immense amount of time and stress and will ensure your affairs remain in the hands of qualified and trained professionals. Finally, don't hire the wrong quarterback, as noted in the next rule. Avoid family members and friends if at all possible and make sure to perform the same level of due diligence when hiring a quarterback in order to make sure they are the right fit to service your planning needs in an independent and competent fashion.

Rule 6: Know who not to hire.

Athletes must do what they feel is best when hiring their team of advisors, as long as that does not include hiring advisors who may not be able to serve their interests effectively. I've already explained a bit about why it's a bad idea to hire family members as advisors, but you should also be aware that there are several other groups you should avoid when selecting advisors.

First, let me give you some more information to consider in regard to hiring family members to serve in one of those key advisory roles—an all-too-common practice that I consider to be one of the biggest mistakes a professional athlete can make. And yet I run into it almost daily.

Many athletes believe they are able to give back financially to a family member by hiring them to serve in an advisory capacity, regardless of whether he or she is qualified for the job. There are a number of athletes who are extremely protective of their upbringing and of those who were there when they had nothing. The way they see it, no one gave them anything, except for this small group of people who were there when they had nothing but a dream. Loyalty means more than anything to those athletes, and they desperately want to take care of the people who helped them.

Others choose to hire family members because it's easy compared to the rigorous, drawn-out process of hiring outside advisors. You know the person you are hiring. There is an established relationship and, hopefully, a level of trust. They are around you constantly, addressing any concerns related to accessibility that can arise with other advisors.

Hiring a family member as a professional advisor raises a number of flags that often lead to serious problems. I have worked with several clients who hired family members to serve as their advisors, and the two sides no longer speak to each other. One or both was challenging to work with, or jealousy became a chronic source of conflict.

It is more than likely that your family members are not qualified to serve in an advisory capacity. Your goal at the start of your journey should be to hire a team of qualified, independent, third-party advisors whom you can trust. In certain circumstances, there are some family members who are more than qualified to manage a player's financial, legal, or tax affairs. Maybe your brother-in-law is a stockbroker or your cousin is an attorney.

That doesn't mean it is a good idea. If someone in your family is qualified to serve in an advisory role, it is preferable that they oversee the person who has been hired to manage that task. If your mom is a successful and qualified estate planning attorney, ask that she oversee your legal advisor for estate planning. In this case, she is able to stay involved without necessarily actually performing the work.

More often than not, those family members, however experienced they may be, have not gone through the due diligence process that you, under any and all circumstances, must rely upon as you hire nonfamily member advisors. Due diligence and background checks are an important way to assure you have assembled a team that represents your values, your personality, your temperament, your interests, and your long-term objectives. Just because someone is family doesn't mean they meet a single one of those requirements.

There is also an inherent jealousy factor. If you hire your cousin to serve as your legal advisor, he may feel threatened any time a credible third party with a greater degree of skill and knowledge enters the picture, and would likely balk at the idea of letting that person into the circle for the benefit of the team. This situation is especially true when your family member may see you as an important source of their income, making them understandably cautious of outsiders threatening to step in and take over. If they are no longer relevant, they may lose the income they have grown dependent on. As a result, they may offer advice and suggestions that are in their best interest, not yours.

You will likely expect your family members to do favors for you, and they are going to expect that they will be doing more work for you than they would for someone else. They may criticize your unreasonable expectations or question how much you value their efforts. Family members can quickly become resentful.

If none of your family members are qualified to serve in an advisory capacity and you remain adamant about including them as part of your team, offer to hire them to screen marketing deals, help out with a specific business opportunity, serve on your charitable board, and so forth.

I will never pass judgment on a client for choosing to give back to his family. I highly recommend giving back in a thoughtful and productive way. But transferring over the power to handle legal, tax, investment, and business consulting may compromise the power of a truly independent third party process to handle a client's wealth planning needs.

While family members sit atop the "do not hire" list, they aren't alone. In the pool of possible player advisors are a number of individuals who, though highly qualified, should be avoided at all costs: fans. I attend games, celebrate big wins, and send congratulatory notes in recognition of postseason honors. Those are gestures you would extend to any business partner or client. Anything more may come across as fan behavior, and good advisors will typically keep those behaviors tempered. Athletes can sniff out a fan and know when an advisor has crossed the line.

I have observed advisors engage clients and potential clients in conversation, heaping praise and admiration onto players. They may make comments such as, "2003 was a phenomenal year for you. I can't believe you had twenty-five tackles." Many athletes may not mind talking about their performance, but they ultimately want their advisors to stay focused on serving their affairs.

While conversing with their advisors, athletes, to a degree, forget that they are successful celebrities. For the advisor, that is part of your goal as well. We want our clients to forget they are celebrities. If they are constantly reminded of their status as an elite athlete, a superiority factor between player and advisor begins to emerge and the relationship becomes difficult to manage. Advisors must establish a level of authority and credibility with their clients, both of which are immediately compromised when the advisor takes on the mentality of a fan or when the athlete's ego manages the relationship.

Some advisors find it difficult to avoid crossing that line. They may attend events such as celebrity golf tournaments that are teeming with sports legends, hall of famers, and athletes they have admired during childhood. This is not to say advisors can't appreciate a particular venue and respect the athletic accomplishments of the client or their peers, but the minute an advisor becomes too much of a fan and forgets how to interact with a client at a professional level, it is hard to pull the client back into a productive professional relationship.

Celebrity wannabes are another group to avoid. Advisors, like professional athletes, are hurled into situations in which they are suddenly dealing with an amazing amount of power, influence, fame, and fortune. It can be extremely fast-paced and sexy, and some advisors get caught up in the scene and start to think that they, too, are celebrities. Again, that type of behavior or misconception crosses a dangerous line. When advisors become overly wrapped up in the celebrity scene, they may lose sight of their purpose, which is to provide sound independent business, legal, financial, and tax advice to their clients. They believe that by being in a club with their clients until 2:00 AM, they are building a professional relationship. Of course, on special occasions, an advisor may be in those situations. However, if these occasions become regular, an otherwise successful advisor could compromise the relationship. There are several different types of personalities in the business, but the advisors who are more likely to build a successful, long-term relationship are those who are in the shadows. You know they exist, but they rarely try to share the spotlight.

I had one client tell me he fired his investment broker after his broker decided to stay out all night with him and was in no condition to wake up the next morning to check the investment markets and the status of his money accordingly. This may seem harsh, but in reality, my client felt the investment broker should have joined up with his client on the weekend when the markets were closed to stay on top of the job he was paid to perform.

There is one final group of advisors you should avoid—the "yes men." Some advisors fear saying no to a client will pose a threat to the client-advisor relationship. They worry that disappointing a client by discouraging him from making a business investment, for example, will serve to upset him and, in turn, destroy the relationship. However, the moment your advisor says yes for fear you will fire him, that is the time to find another advisor.

A professional athlete must seek out advisors who are willing to say no when there is a compelling reason to do so, even if they know full well that it could upset the client and jeopardize the relationship. An athlete needs an advisor who will stand by his professional opinions when it is in the best interest of the client. As a client, you should respect the opinions of your advisors—they are professionals, after all—and admire them for sticking to their guns in the face of opposition.

This is the only way I do business. I have all the numbers related to my clients' budget, income, debt, personal savings goals, assets, insurance, companies, and so forth. If one of my clients approaches me about purchasing a $200,000 car and that purchase will have a negative effect toward certain lifestyle or savings goals, I'm not afraid to convey that message with clear reasoning. I may offer alternatives. For example, perhaps a $100,000 car is more reasonable. If a purchase fits within the client's discretionary spending budget, there may be no reason for me to advise against it. But if a client approaches me about a purchase and my response is simply, "Go for it. You had a great season," the client is given no confidence in the accuracy or value of my advice because there is no evidence to support it.

I like to present numbers to illustrate how a major purchase will affect an athlete's budget. Whether my client wants to hear it or not, those numbers show that my analysis of the situation is based on hard facts. For example, if an athlete expects me to agree to every business investment, the risk falls on me. I am getting paid to provide independent advice and guidance, and if I am not willing to be honest about a transaction or investment and the deal blows up, I'm failing to perform the job I was hired to do.

Athletes should understand that advisors are there to guide them through the wealth planning and business planning process and provide advice that they believe to be in their best interest. Some advisors are self-serving and may not always have the athlete's best interest at heart. Other advisors may be financially conservative and decide to impose their risk tolerance on your investment decisions. But the majority of advisors are there to help you meet your savings and wealth planning goals, and getting to that point requires that the advisor is willing to say no.

It is equally important that you, the athlete, avoid becoming the "yes man." Do not be led to believe that you have to acquiesce to everything your advisors say. Otherwise, you set a precedent, and eventually everyone around you is making decisions for you and you're just being pulled around without any voice in the matter. Assert your opinions, risk tolerance, and objectives clearly so your advisors take your position into account before taking action. A thoughtful advisor will listen to and educate his or her client as much as possible when discussing such decisions so all parties move forward together.

Rule 7: Understand the fee structure of an advisory team.

A problem that often surfaces in athlete-advisor relationships is a misconception that advisors make a lot more money than is actually the case. An investment broker or advisor rarely if ever collects a fee more than approximately 1 to 1.5 percent of the total value of a client's assets invested with that broker or investment advisor. For example, an investment broker or advisor managing approximately $1 million for a client may collect $10,000 to $15,000 per year as a fee.

A CPA may charge between $700 to $20,000 and up to prepare and file tax returns. Much of this depends on how many returns are necessary and the complexity of the return. For example, if an athlete is operating a business with different subsidiaries along with multiple partners, the returns will require more work and analysis.

Insurance products, such as life insurance, annuities, and disability policies, pay commissions that can be substantial or minimal. Typically, the insurance agent or advisor is paid a commission from the insurance company directly. Certain insurance advisors are fee based, which means they are paid a fee by the athlete directly and do not accept commissions from the insurance company.

Attorneys charge an hourly fee that can range from $150 to $1000 per hour depending on the nature of the legal representation and the jurisdiction. Attorneys may also charge a flat fee for certain projects.

Your marketing consultant will collect about 15 percent of any endorsement contract, and your agent will collect about 3 to 4 percent of your team salary.

The fees you pay to your advisors should directly correlate with the level of service you receive, from education to face-to-face meetings. Be mindful, however, that the fees you pay represent only a fraction of an advisor's annual income.

If you intend on surrounding yourself with a team of qualified and competent advisors, realize that it can be costly. That can, at times, be difficult for an athlete to understand, considering that most athletes are not used to paying fees for all these services. A business owner is more familiar with the amount and type of fees paid to attorneys, CPAs, business consultants, and so forth, as part of their risk management process and ongoing business needs.

Boselli says that athletes should not be afraid to pay for these services, as it will pay off in the long run when you have a competent team reviewing your deals and making sure your financial, legal, business, and tax matters are handled in coordination. "It will cost you a little bit," he says. "But especially those guys who are first-rounders, they've got plenty of money, and I think it will save them money and make them money."[8]

Chapter 4

Use Wealth Planning
to Secure Your Future

Tax, legal, and financial planning are all valuable tools that serve to address the array of issues related to an athlete's personal finances during the course of his or her career and retirement. Those tools become more effective when used in concert with one another for the purposes of preserving wealth, sustaining business opportunities, and even estate planning to address an athlete's goals, interests, priorities, concerns, and risks. A unified plan, as opposed to a fragmented plan, promotes accountability among advisors and ensures all risks and objectives are addressed.

Your advisors should work cooperatively to maximize your asset protection and wealth preservation needs through a combination of strategies. A carefully organized and executed wealth plan will preserve your finances through not only tax planning but careful legal planning and financial planning as well. The process will guide you toward insurance policies that will serve to mitigate risks to your assets and corporate structures that help you protect, manage, and control your business interests. It will carefully outline the distribution of your assets to your spouse, parents, children, and others through an estate plan. And it will consider your risk tolerance and personal values in devising an investment portfolio that produces a maximum return.

Though the grunt work related to wealth planning appears to fall in the hands of your advisory team, you must take ownership in your wealth plan as well. Commit to educate yourself about various strategies and terminology, and make sure to communicate your wealth planning goals, personal values, and risk tolerance related to investments. The following rules will help athletes manage the various risks confronting their financial security and will enable long-term preservation of assets and opportunities presented during their career.

Rule 1: Address tax planning as a component of wealth preservation.

Most Americans receive evidence of last year's reportable income from the W-2 forms issued by their employer or from 1099 forms or other tax-related forms at the start of a new year. Typically, we turn them over to our CPA and wash our hands of the matter for another year.

Taxes take on new meaning when you begin to collect six-, seven-, or eight-figure salaries. What once was a yearly nuisance can now require intensive tax planning. And yet one of the biggest challenges I encounter in working with young athletes at the start of their careers is a failure to recognize the importance of tax planning and reporting as an integral component of wealth planning.

In too many instances, an athlete enters the league, collects his paycheck, and deposits it in the bank, never contacting a CPA until taxes are due the following year. That approach can be costly, and such costs may be avoided through competent tax advice and planning. Tax planning is a critical aspect of managing your wealth. For example, there are certain tax savings you may realize when your income is paid to a corporation or to a partnership you own. Furthermore, unnecessary state taxes on endorsement deals, federal and state taxes from various investment losses or earnings, and surprise alternative minimum tax as the result of a particular municipal bond portfolio can all be avoided and managed through proper tax planning prior to you receiving the first team or endorsement paycheck.

Engage a tax specialist who is not only responsible for preparing tax returns but also looking at complex tax issues from a holistic perspective. Of equal importance is hiring a tax advisor who understands the tax and accounting issues related to professional athletics. Most individuals file income tax returns in the state in which they live and work. Professional athletes, however, travel to several states and even countries for games and earn income in each of those locations, which requires multiple state income tax returns or complex international tax planning. In addition, if athletes collect endorsement or marketing income outside of the United States, they have to deal with international tax issues as well.

Numerous factors influence an individual's final decision as to which state he should claim residency in, and tax issues are at the top of that list. Income tax rates vary from state to state. Several states, including Florida, Texas, and Nevada, do not assess state income tax. As a result, if you play for an NFL team in Florida, you will not have to pay state income tax in Florida for income earned in Florida. Not having to pay state income tax is a cost savings to an athlete.

There are numerous tax issues related to investments and financial planning. As your career evolves, tax planning can save you substantial money as it relates to your investment choices and elections. For example, working with your investment broker to harvest tax losses from your investments that lost money at the end of the year or to explore certain types of bonds that will reduce the amount of tax you owe on the income generated from those bonds is critical.

Bad tax planning can cost you substantial money as well. Thus, it is imperative you make sure to hire a qualified and reputable CPA that not only just reacts to your tax needs but also provides proactive guidance in order to plan for certain costs or expenses accordingly, whether expected or not. There is nothing worse than being surprised by your CPA and told that you owe the IRS a large sum of money due to underpayment, unexpected income, or errors—especially when you haven't set the money aside or your money is tied up in other assets.

Most of my clients were unaware of federal estate taxes before they came into wealth. They were in for an unpleasant surprise. Combined with state estate or inheritance taxes, federal estate taxes can drive significant decisions relating to residency, wealth creation, ownership of assets, trust planning, insurance needs, and planned giving. Based on current law in April of 2010, there is no estate tax owed upon the death of a married couple or a single person in 2010. However, estate tax is back in 2011 at a 55 percent tax rate upon death of an individual with an estate worth more than $1 million or a married couple with an estate worth more than $2 million. The potential cost of not planning for estate taxes can unnecessarily cost your family and your legacy a significant amount of money. Many successful athletes will be faced with tens of millions of dollars in estate taxes in 2011 and beyond under current law.[1] Certain states also assess a state estate or inheritance tax, adding to the total cost. In these circumstances, changing residency to another state may save additional estate taxes.

Many young people don't take the time to bother with estate taxes since many of them think they will live forever. However, once you come into wealth and significant income, you need to plan for your unexpected death or disability in order to make sure your money and assets are transferred to the appropriate people or charities and are protected during the process. Due to the significant cost of various federal estate taxes and state inheritance/estate taxes, you must sit down with a qualified attorney and make sure you are structuring your estate properly to reduce potential estate taxes. Properly titled assets, your state of residency, trust planning, charitable transfers and business entity planning all have a big impact on the amount of estate taxes you will owe upon death.

Tax planning will play an even more pivotal role in wealth management and asset preservation as your career progresses. Endorsement contracts and other sources of compensation may supplement your player salary. You may decide to set up a company and support your family through your company payroll for services rendered. Each strategy carries its own tax implications, and each player's wealth planning goals will further influence his tax plan.

You will optimize your potential for success by engaging a tax advisor early in your career. Furthermore, your tax advisor should be an independent advisor and not part of your investment advisor's office or agent's office. Tax planning and preparation is a specific skill that should be handled by an independent firm or CPA who specializes in tax preparation and planning.

Rule 2: Communicate your risk tolerance and personal values in order to guide your investment planning.

Wealthy individuals have an endless selection of investment options before them. For your investment strategy to be successful, you must not only be working in a partnership with a trustworthy and knowledgeable investment advisor, you also need to take ownership in your investment activities. Educate yourself as to the options before you and effectively communicate your goals, interests, priorities, risk tolerance, and values, all of which will play a pivotal role in the investment process.

There are several guiding forces behind an athlete's investment portfolio, the most obvious being the savings objectives, rate of return, and amount of risk you are willing to take to achieve a potential rate of return. An experienced investment advisor will be able to select an investment strategy that takes into consideration how much you need to live on in the future, as well as analyzing how much you need to invest today based on inflation and your risk tolerance.

Your risk tolerance will provide your advisor with further guidance in selecting investment options for your portfolio. Some investments are extremely risky with the potential for an even higher rate of return, while others are considered low risk with not much promise of a significant return on your investment. An experienced financial advisor will determine an athlete's risk tolerance based on their responses to a number of questions, and review those responses to create an investment portfolio that balances the athlete's risk tolerance.

I have worked with some athletes, however, whose investment philosophies are inconsistent. Those athletes indicate a low-risk tolerance for certain investment allocations, but then invest in high-risk business opportunities. Some may decide to invest their signing bonus entirely into a low-risk money market fund, but then engage in an aggressive business plan. Be mindful of your risk tolerance and exercise that same level of caution with all your investments. Follow the guidance of your advisors, who will coordinate those objectives with investment options aimed at generating the greatest return. There will be times when you and your advisors will need to be aggressive and times when you will need to be conservative. Balancing those occasions and the timing of those decisions in certain planning areas are critical.

There are countless ways to invest your money, and there are ways of doing it that reflect your values and principles through what is known as social investing. Some of my clients are extremely cognizant of environmental issues. I work with certain athletes who buy hybrid cars and will not invest in companies that emit pollutants into the environment. Derrick Brooks doesn't drink alcohol and, as a result, has made the conscious decision to not invest in alcohol production or supply companies. You may earn a strong return by investing in oil company stock, but if you don't believe in their mission, it would seem to be an unwise investment.

Some of my clients don't care how a company makes money; they want to invest in whatever companies will give them the highest rate of return. However, if you are concerned about where your investment dollars are being allocated based on certain social objections, your values need to be communicated to your advisors and taken into consideration.

Regardless of which approach is right for you, it is imperative you understand your investment principles and make sure your advisors commit to your objectives. Be wary if your financial advisor never asks you questions to determine exactly what drives your investment decisions and risk tolerance.

Rule 3: Avoid potential investment scams by requesting a qualified third party review of your investment holdings.

There are many qualified and honest investment advisors serving clients every day. However, most of us hear about advisors who stole, cheated, or misled clients into believing their money was safely invested. Until recently, many investors assumed their money was safe when they hired a reputable and experienced investment advisor or firm to invest their money. When the Madoff and Stanford scandals hit in 2009, many investors were alarmed at how easily they were misled and wondered how such fraud could have taken place without anyone knowing.[2]

Not all fraud can be detected. However, I highly encourage all of our clients to hire a third-party investment or financial firm to review and analyze their investment statements. Such a review will uncover the fees being charged by their investment advisor and whether the advisor is also receiving commissions for trades or other services. In addition, such a review will make sure your risk tolerance is reflected in the current investment allocation and whether certain stocks, bonds, or other securities are appropriate at any given time considering your investment horizon, risk tolerance, and wealth planning goals.

In order to help deter fraud, hiring a third party to review your investment statements will uncover whether you are invested in nonpublicly traded firms (e.g., Stanford) and/or whether your investment advisor can provide you an independent third-party custodian report (e.g. Madoff). A custodian report should be an independent third-party accounting of your investment accounts and should match your investment advisor's statement of your investment accounts. Investing your money can be overwhelming, but with proper checks and balances and an understanding of how the business works, you will be much more comfortable with your investment approach. It will cost you money to have someone review your investment advisor's statements, but the cost pales in comparison to the alternatives in the event you lose most or all of your investments due to fraud, misrepresentation, or miscommunicating your risk tolerance.

Rule 4: Hire a legal advisor to plan for the worst-case scenario.

Tax and investment planning tends to bleed over into the legal issues surrounding wealth management. The two sides work closely to develop strategies, approve transactions, and ensure a client's wealth management efforts from all three pillars—tax, legal, and financial planning—are organized.

Legal planning, similar to tax planning, tends to be underemphasized among young athletes because most operate under the false assumption that they only need an attorney if they get into trouble. Young athletes are especially likely to underestimate the value of a legal advisor if their agent happens to be an attorney. Even if your agent is an attorney—many are, in fact—that does not mean he is qualified to handle transactional work such as asset protection, business transactions, estate planning, prenuptial planning, corporation or partnership planning, and an endless list of other legal matters that surface during and after a professional athlete's career. Your attorney, like your CPA, should be a specialist, someone who is an expert in these areas. The legal issues you face will be in flux throughout the course of your career as your personal and professional needs change. Having a qualified legal team in place from the onset of your career will help you navigate those issues and help educate you so that any contingencies—you are named in a lawsuit, for example—can be met with a legal strategy relevant to your individual situation.

As an attorney, I am always working to ensure there are options on the table in the event that a worst-case scenario becomes reality. When a client calls and asks us to screen a business deal, I often find myself saying after a review of the financials, "This looks great. But if for some reason it fails, what is our recourse?" Nobody wants to hear that, and a client usually brushes it off by explaining that his business partner is an ex-teammate or that the deal is just a handshake and can easily be undone.

I often find myself playing the role of the bad guy in those situations, telling my clients what they don't want to hear. But as their advisor, it is my job to be ever-mindful of the worst-case scenario and plan for it. Performing background checks of business partners, reviewing operating agreements to determine if you will be required to invest more money in the company if the company needs the funds, understanding to what extent you are personally guaranteeing debts of the company, determining how your interests will be valued upon your death or disability, dispute resolution, tax allocations, control and voting—all these are issues that you need an experienced attorney to review on your behalf before investing a single penny into a business deal. It will cost you money, but it will potentially save you more money down the road and provide you peace of mind.

Rule 5: Create a detailed estate plan.

One of your estate planning attorney's primary functions will be to establish and oversee your estate plan, which sets forth to whom and how your assets (cash, real estate, jewelry, cars, business interests, insurance proceeds, investments, etc.) will be managed and distributed upon your death or disability.

It may seem premature to have that discussion when you are a young and single rookie without children. Derrick Brooks said his first estate plan was rudimentary and included a single document that dictated how his assets should be distributed to his family members upon his death. It changed as he got older, married, and had children. During his early years in the NFL, however, he said the time wasn't right for him to implement a wealth preservation plan, simply because he didn't understand the intricacies behind it.

Without an estate plan, state law will dictate how your assets will be distributed upon your death. By hiring a good legal team, however, you can create an estate plan that will distribute your assets under your terms, potentially keep your affairs private, and also address potential federal estate tax issues that can cost your family millions of dollars. Your attorney can help identify and manage how your assets will be distributed upon your death, protect your assets from future creditors, provide for charitable gifts, and provide access to money to pay potential estate taxes.

Upon death or disability, your estate can be distributed entirely to your family, but how it is distributed is addressed on an individual basis. As a young rookie, you may designate your parents or siblings as the sole benefactors of your estate. That may change, however, if you marry and change your estate plan, designating your spouse as the beneficiary. The implications behind that, however, are that your wife may remarry after collecting an inheritance and then later divorce. At that point, her ex-husband may be entitled to a portion of your estate. Or, she may marry someone with children and then draft a will indicating that her stepchildren will inherit her estate. Those and similar situations demonstrate that regardless of your intentions, your estate could end up in the hands of strangers unless an estate plan is properly drafted and executed.

Children add another dimension to an already complex plan. If your wife is the sole benefactor and you and your wife die together, your entire estate may transfer to your children. You must add some sense of control to that transfer unless you want your children and their spouses to come into all of your money at once. I have yet to see a case in which a young person comes into a sizable inheritance and makes wise spending, savings, and investment decisions. In my opinion, under no circumstances should all of your money be distributed outright to your children. Rather, it should be held in trusts and managed by trustees. There are countless ways to draft an estate plan to address this type of structure, and every successful athlete owes it to himself and his family to be fully educated as to the available options.

If your estate plan is drafted appropriately, it can promote social responsibility within your family. Your children can be encouraged to do something worthwhile in their lives without ever having to worry about working just to make money. The flexibility and freedom afforded to your family from a properly structured estate plan is powerful when you consider how they will be able to impact their community, profession, and family when they don't have to make decisions based on money.

You may also choose to leave a portion of your estate, or the entire estate, to a nonprofit organization—your own private foundation, a hospital, church, or your alma mater, for instance. Your estate can build a lasting legacy in your memory and continue to support your vision and principles years after your death.

You cannot have an estate plan without an asset protection plan, and you can't have an asset protection plan without an estate plan. The two are intertwined. If you are worth $20 million, you must have a plan in place to protect those assets from creditors or from someone who tries to sue you for any number of reasons. It can become an even bigger issue upon your death. A creditor may come out of the woodwork and claim you breached a contract on a business investment and owe him $5 million. I am referring to unscrupulous creditors, creditors with illegitimate claims, or third-party creditors that are simply trying to find deep pockets to satisfy judgments.

Because athletes are wealthy, they are a target for many people and companies looking to access their money. As a result, you need to protect your assets and your estate from people making false or exaggerated claims. You would be amazed at how many people will try to take advantage of your family upon your death by suing your estate or beneficiaries based on meritless claims. As a result, asset protection is a critical aspect of wealth planning for you and your family during your life and upon your death. Without an asset protection plan, the burden and responsibility to defend such actions and potentially satisfy any judgments fall squarely in the lap of your family.

A prenuptial agreement should be considered as part of your estate plan and risk management plan, as well. For an athlete earning a substantial income, you have to be aware of the fact that there are people in the world who are after your money. You may find yourself in a relationship that you believe to be genuine, when in reality the other party is simply looking for financial security. On the other hand, professional athletes travel frequently and attract a great deal of attention. Temptations are endless. That lifestyle can strain a marriage, and many unfortunately end in divorce. Prenuptial agreements can take away from the romance of a budding relationship, but you must accept the real possibility that a marriage can end and, without a prenuptial agreement, can severely alter your financial situation.

A divorce in the absence of a prenuptial agreement means your assets and future income will be split in some fashion with your ex-spouse. Your assets can then end up in the hands of that person's second or third spouse or stepchildren, affecting the future inheritance of your children or, if you remarry, your future spouse. I have worked with cases in which, because of multiple divorces and remarriages, my client's earnings are in the hands of people for whom they were never intended. Make sure to explore the use of a prenuptial agreement prior to marriage in order to protect your wealth from unforeseen risks. A carefully drafted prenuptial agreement will also make sure to not conflict with your estate plan in order to preserve the intended distribution of your assets upon your death.

Rule 6: Address your increase in risk through insurance planning.

Insurance planning is a component of a sound financial, estate, and tax plan, which can provide cash benefits to your family to pay taxes, pay off debts, or provide additional income for them to support each other in the event of your death or disability. There are many types of insurance policies. Some are designed to simply pay your family a certain amount of money upon your death. Some insurance policies are designed to provide money to your business partners so they have cash to purchase your business interests upon death. Some of my clients secure "key man coverage." Should one of my client's key employees die unexpectedly, money from an insurance policy will finance the hiring of a replacement or cushion his company from any resulting loss in revenue.

Liability insurance is valuable for any professional athlete who operates youth camps in the off-season or needs to insure the value of their cars, jewelry, homes, boats, and so on. Some more exotic insurance policies, such as kidnapping and ransom insurance, are often applicable for certain athletes who travel overseas or have been subject to certain types of threats. Furthermore, certain types of insurance policies provide protection from identity theft and will help the recovery process.

Disability coverage is a necessity for any professional athlete who engages in a contact sport, where injury over the course of his career is not only possible but probable. Should you, as a pro athlete, suffer an injury during a game, practice, or training session, your disability policy will provide a source of income during the period of time you are unable to compete and collect a salary. Similarly, an amateur prospect can secure coverage that will protect him should he be injured anytime before draft day.

On the other hand, life insurance planning should not be approached with a specific insurance product in mind. Rather, it should be approached from a financial, legal, and tax planning perspective. If, upon your death, your estate tax is projected to be $4 million, you must find a way for your family to pay that $4-million tax bill. Your advisory team should explore incorporating life insurance as a potential tool within your estate plan to help provide your family the financial means to cover potential taxes and provide them the necessary financial means to maintain their lifestyle.

Initially, you should take a very conservative and thoughtful approach to insurance as a wealth planning tool. That is especially relevant for athletes whose playing days are limited. Make sure to ask whether the death benefit provided by the life insurance is guaranteed or not. An insurance agent will typically sell you a life insurance policy in order to provide your family with a sum of money upon your death. However, certain types of life insurance policies will not guarantee that your family will receive this sum of money upon your death. If making sure that a certain sum of money is available to your family upon your death, make sure that your agent is selling you a guaranteed death benefit life insurance product and ask to which age the death benefit is guaranteed. Otherwise, you may pay premiums for a benefit that won't be there when you need it.

Make sure the life insurance carrier issuing the life insurance is well capitalized and highly rated in order to meet the promised obligations. Make sure the life insurance is properly owned. In most cases, you do not want to own the life insurance personally; rather, an irrevocable trust should own the policy in order to remove the value of the life insurance death benefit from your estate. For example, if you are worth $10 million and personally acquire a $10 million life insurance policy, for estate tax purposes you are worth $20 million. As a result, your family might unnecessarily pay estate taxes on $20 million versus estate taxes on $10 million. By working with an attorney to properly set up an irrevocable trust to own the policy, you may avoid the additional estate taxes and make sure your family receives the entire $10 million in death benefits free of federal estate tax.

When considering various insurance needs, make sure to work with an advisor who has experience securing insurance coverage for the professional athlete marketplace. Relationships with insurance carriers and the reinsurance marketplace are critical if an advisor will be successful securing coverage. Those relationships are not spontaneous but rather are developed over time. That is reason enough to hire an insurance professional familiar with this specialized market, rather than working through an inexperienced family member or friend who has no experience in this planning area.

Some life insurance carriers contract with separate reinsurance companies to assume some of the risks associated with insuring professional athletes. Due to the recent controversy surrounding performance enhancement drugs, the few remaining reinsurance companies in the life insurance marketplace have tightened access to coverage, causing significant impact on athletes' ability to secure life insurance. The reinsurance companies review and underwrite athletes on a case-by-case basis with a strict eye toward whether the athletes are taking or have taken performance enhancement drugs. As a result, athletes' access to life insurance coverage is now restricted.

Typically, healthy nonathletes can obtain life insurance coverage from insurers and reinsurers at most levels. But professional athletes have encountered difficulties recently because of concerns from the industry regarding not just lifestyle issues but concentration of risk as well. For example, most insurance companies don't want to insure more than a few athletes on any one team due to the potential payout upon a catastrophic accident. For example, consider the potential life insurance payout resulting from a plane crash carrying a football team to their road game. If the insurance company has insured a number of these players, the payout could be in the hundreds of millions, a sum that may cripple the insurance company financially. As a result, reinsurers will not only conduct a background check on an athlete but monitor coverage based on how many current players they insure on any one team.

The issue is further complicated by the fact that professional sports teams will occasionally take out insurance policies on their players so that, should one of the players die unexpectedly, the insurance policy will pay the team enough money (sometimes more than they need) to cover the remainder of the player's guaranteed payments under contract. Most athletes don't realize that certain teams are using a portion of the athlete's insurance capacity, affecting an athlete's ability to obtain that insurance for his estate or family needs.

I always recommend athletes secure life insurance coverage while they are young because of unknown health risks and problems down the road from playing professional sports. In addition, public image issues among a very few professional athletes have only served to negatively affect the reputation of pro athletes, further convincing reinsurers of the need to more carefully scrutinize their underwriting.

Rule 7: Use a budget to control your personal spending.

It's easy for a young athlete to get caught up in the celebrity world and all it encompasses, from fast cars and large homes to designer clothes and luxury vacations. It can often lead to uncontrolled personal spending. Most athletes aren't looking at receipts and tracking expenses.

What players often don't realize, however, is how quickly the earnings from their multimillion-dollar salaries can disappear. When you are thrown into a certain lifestyle, it is easy to start spending more than you earn. Now that you're playing Major League Baseball, you're shopping at Neiman Marcus rather than Nordstrom's. You're spending $300 on a shirt rather than $100, and you're buying five of those shirts rather than one or two. Those expenses add up, and suddenly your advisors are calling to break the news that you budgeted $20,000 for clothes but spent $100,000.

As important as estate planning, investments, insurance strategies, and tax planning are to your financial health, your day-to-day spending is what can creep up on you and threaten the long-term success of your wealth plan. It is particularly dangerous for an athlete whose lucrative contract will be a thing of the past if an injury keeps him sidelined or ends his career. Harnessing out-of-control spending habits will prevent the situation from spiraling out of control, causing significant damage to your financial health.

One of the first pieces of advice handed to Eric Steinbach after he was drafted in 2003 was simple: Not all professional athletes are set for life with the income they will earn through their first pro contract. Should an unexpected occurrence bring your playing career to an end, you would likely be forced to get a job.

"For the first four years of my career, which was the extension of my contract, I lived below my means," Steinbach says. He bought a reasonably priced townhouse and reached an agreement with a Cincinnati car dealership that provided him with a car. "I kept my spending to a minimum. I went on vacation and treated myself here and there, but I didn't go out and buy four cars and two houses."[3]

Establishing a budget with your advisors is a tedious, time-consuming, unpleasant task that requires you to plan all of your expenses, from groceries to entertainment. Some of my clients follow a very strict budget, which requires that they monitor every penny spent. One of my clients budgets the amount of money he will spend on gasoline for his car. When he begins to exceed his monthly budget, he won't fill up his tank. At the other end of the spectrum are athletes who wouldn't know if $100,000 was missing from their accounts.

Unlike other wealth management issues in which financial, legal, insurance, and tax professionals are on hand to oversee every finite detail, the bulk of the responsibility for budgeting is in your hands. If the primary goal of your wealth plan is to have $10 million of cash in the bank when you retire, you must follow the budget as designed by you and your advisors. Athletes who are more cognizant of their budget and the value of money preserve their wealth over a longer period of time and are more successful in building a pot of money for their retirement.

Setting and abiding by a monthly spending budget will establish guideposts that drive your financial forecasting and help you in evaluating the effectiveness of your advisory team and its ability to manage your wealth issues. If you follow a budget and still fall behind in your savings goals, you should look to your advisors to determine whether the investment structures they have implemented are appropriate.

On the other hand, if an athlete ignores his budget and then questions his advisors about what happened to his money, it's easy for those advisors to shift the blame. At the end of the year, a budget that is carefully planned and executed is a critical step in understanding where your money was spent and whether you are falling over or under budget in certain spending categories. A budget analysis will allow for modifications and adjustments in the coming year, and allow you to evaluate your spending habits. If you followed your budget, but efforts to achieve your long-term savings goals are failing, you need to turn to your advisors for answers.

Some of our clients have turned to us for assistance in monitoring the spending habits of their family members, realizing that a budget does not start and end with their own spending. Derrick Brooks has established a budget for his entire family and allocates a predetermined amount of money to his family on a monthly basis. It can be hard to start pinching pennies with your spouse, though, particularly for those athletes who married after achieving professional success, as their spouses are accustomed to the lifestyle and income of a professional athlete.

One of my clients helped his wife open a Neiman Marcus credit card under the stipulation that she exercise discretion in her purchases. However, my staff found that her charges at Neiman Marcus had exceeded $20,000 a month over several months. I was in a precarious situation, but we immediately informed the client about his wife's spending and its effect on the family's budget. I called him and explained the situation. He spoke with his wife, and they both agreed to cut up the card.

Living under a budget does not mean you shouldn't enjoy your financial success. Many of my clients design their wealth plans in a way that allows them to do nice things for themselves, their families, and other people in their lives, which I believe is of the utmost importance. I don't want my clients to reflect on their careers and say, "I'm successful. I've made it. I'm one of the few who can play at the professional level. So I'm going to sit around and worry about my money and not do anything with it." Such an approach will likely backfire over time. The key is to understand the impact of certain purchases and the effect they may or may not have on your long-term savings goals. I always tell my clients that I want them to enjoy basically the same lifestyle they are accustomed to now when they are sixty. Not only will they thank me when they are sixty and are able to travel, play golf, help their family, and not worry about money, but they will look back and appreciate the time and money they spent building their financial plan.

Enjoy your success. But always remain in control of your budget and keep in mind to balance those expenses with realistic goals regarding your future wealth management needs.

Rule 8: Educate yourself.

By reading this book, you've already taken a big step toward educating yourself. Some rookie athletes enter the big leagues having spent their entire lives tucking money under a mattress or, at best, depositing it in a checking account. That changes when you sign a contract for a million-dollar salary.

Your newfound wealth comes with many decisions on what to do with it, decisions that are hard to make when you don't know the first thing about investments and money management.

The advice you receive, particularly related to financial planning, is only as good as the information you provide your advisors, making education all the more valuable. If you hire a financial advisor to manage your investments, it is up to you to convey your goals and objectives. Perhaps you want to retire in five years with all liquid assets. That information is important for suitability purposes and for your advisor to determine how prudent your investment strategy will be. However, you will not be able to effectively communicate that information if you have no understanding of the terminology and the options that investment planning affords.

Derrick Brooks says his early financial decisions were driven by fear over the fact that he had such a sizable amount of money with no idea of what he should do with it. He had no experience with or knowledge of investments, and left his earnings in a money market account for a full year—which may have been a missed opportunity, he acknowledges, given that the stock market was booming. "I said to myself, 'An educated dollar made more money over time than a quick, uneducated dollar,'" he says. "So I had to educate my dollar, and I don't regret that decision."[4]

In his early years in the NFL, Brooks attended weekly seminars at a financial services company in order to learn about mutual funds, estate taxes, and other financial issues that he would be faced with over the course of his career.

One of my clients, after receiving his signing bonus, spent a month researching investments, bonds, stocks, the structure of investment houses, and various other business topics, and learned the terminology associated with each. He dedicated a significant amount of time to learning about a world that, until he was drafted, was completely foreign.

Another client spent his off-season working as an unpaid intern for Merrill Lynch. His payoff was gaining knowledge and insight into the business from an insider's point of view with the help of experienced professionals so that he might be better equipped to handle his personal business matters.

Education outside of the classes offered in college is important to understand the application of certain financial issues in real life. For example, Tony Boselli was a business major at the University of Southern California and says he still had no idea how to decipher portfolio statements and other financial records as an NFL rookie. "Not only that, I was making a ton of money, and I was barely even looking at it," he adds.[5]

My clients who are successful in achieving their wealth management goals know their financial information better than most advisors. That requires more involvement than simply planning and following a budget. They know the status of all of their investments, they know about their current tax and legal issues, and off the tops of their heads they can tell me the names of their companies, their individual values, and the business of the day within each company.

It is imperative that, from the onset of your career, you make the conscious decision to be personally involved in your wealth planning affairs at the highest level possible. Should your advisor retire or leave the business, it is imperative that you know as much if not more about your planning needs and issues so that you can bring a new advisor to the table and educate him as to the various facets of your business affairs and not lose a step toward meeting your long-term objectives.

The education process is invaluable, and an area in which you, the athlete, must take the lead, though your advisors can guide you through the education process. Our job during those first years is to educate our clients.

Boselli says the NFL has taken the initiative in providing players with educational opportunities. But players need to take advantage of those opportunities, he adds. "They offer internships; barely any players take them. They have player programs every week with different speakers; barely anyone shows up except the rookies because they have to, and they don't even listen." The NFL could do more, he admits, but it's up to the players to take the initiative in their own education.[6]

It takes discipline, something to which athletes should be accustomed. As disciplined as you are to work out twice a day and take care of your body, you should be equally committed to your education in the wealth planning arena. Pick up another book, go to the library, or research these topics on the Internet. Be sure to check out the resources I've listed for you in the back of this book. You learn more by doing, but conducting research and learning on your own runs a close second.

Chapter 5

Identify the Risks
in Business Opportunities

Business opportunities, or rather investing cash or signing on debt for ownership in a successful business such as a real estate project, franchise, clothing company, technology company, marketing firm, and so on can be a long-term viable and often lucrative investment option for professional athletes. These types of investments can produce highly profitable returns and serve to diversify an athlete's investment portfolio.

And yet most of my clients will confess they've also been burned through at least one failed business deal. Unfortunately, most deals are not successful—a harsh reality, and a costly one for many investors. Derrick Brooks learned that lesson the hard way early in his career. He and two other athletes wanted to go into business together and agreed to a deal with a friend from college who sold them on the idea of a T-shirt company. Brooks and the other two players handed over $35,000 each. The deal never materialized, and the money was gone.[1]

A former advisor to Tony Boselli presented him with several private business investments over the course of his career, including an option to invest significant money in a fast-food franchise that would produce a profitable return—or so his advisor claimed. In the end, Boselli lost a large sum of money and fired his advisor, who, as he later discovered, had allegedly collected undisclosed "management fees" through the transaction.[2] But Brooks, Boselli, and other athletes who have suffered under failed business arrangements are quick to point out the lessons learned through their experiences. It took them losing money to understand the importance of approaching any business arrangement with a detailed plan.

"I can't thank him enough for that lesson, because it was a long time before I even thought about entering into a business relationship with a family member or a friend after that," Brooks says. "I'm glad it only cost me $35,000. Some guys, it costs them millions."[3]

A professional athlete's time is completely consumed during the course of the season, from games and practices to media interviews and team meetings. That leaves him with the four- to five-month off-season to catch up on the rest of his life, which includes managing existing business opportunities. At the same time, family, friends, advisors, and casual acquaintances will inundate you with business opportunities, from commercial land development to an investment in a start-up company. As a young athlete, you should expect to face these investment decisions during the course of your career. But also recognize that losing money, though common, does not have to happen. It can be avoided in most cases with significant due diligence up front.

The key is to engage a qualified business consultant who is trained and experienced in reviewing the financial, market, and business plan data. This consultant should not be your agent, your investment advisor, or your CPA. Rather, you need to hire a specialized consulting firm that will review the opportunity on its face and give you honest advice regarding the business plan and risk. In addition, they should negotiate and communicate the best deal they can on your behalf. Legal issues surrounding the opportunity are also very important to address up front. This due diligence will cost money. However, if the deal is worth your time, the cost is worth the peace of mind. If the deal is too risky, you will have spent a small amount of professional fees to save yourself not only your potential investment, but potential money owed to banks as a guarantor on any loans associated with the company.

The following rules will help protect athletes and their families from business opportunities that are either fraudulent or high risk, while in the meantime capturing and managing business opportunities that will make money.

Rule 1: Invest in business deals to make money, diversify your portfolio, and create new opportunities.

Business investments present professional athletes with a unique opportunity to get involved in businesses and industries that appeal to their personal interests and with the opportunity to make money. The right business opportunity can produce significant returns and build great value in the long run.

By investing in various business opportunities, you may be better equipped to weather economic downturns, political cycles, and other events that can affect your traditional investments. I always tell my clients to make sure they diversify their business interests so that they are not concentrated in any one sector, market, or region. For example, several of my clients invested in Florida real estate during the early 2000s. Due to concern that the housing boom would end at some point and hit certain areas of the country worse than others, we made sure that our clients diversified their real-estate investments in other states and cities that were less vulnerable to huge market swings. We also made sure that clients strongly considered investing in something other than real estate to avoid having a significant portion of their net worth exposed to an eventual downturn in the real-estate market, as noted in 2007 and 2008.

Investing in business also opens opportunities that otherwise might not present themselves. Through their activities in business deals, my clients have developed relationships with other investors and business leaders who introduce them to people and opportunities in other industries and markets. One of my clients made over six figures in thirty days simply because he was in business with a partner who had access to a quick real-estate opportunity. Without his connection to the investor group, that opportunity would not have existed.

A planning area we spend significant time addressing is how to build a bridge into retirement not just for financial purposes, but with respect to maintaining a sense of self-worth, pride, and confidence following retirement from professional sports. Whether operating a chain of auto dealerships or overseeing a commercial land development project, these business opportunities offers my clients a place to go to work and feel productive in retirement, which is an invaluable benefit.

When an athlete retires, the risk of divorce, depression, dependency, and debt is higher than ever. Once an athlete is no longer playing their sport and all attention, access, camaraderie, and competition disappear, reality sinks in. This is why it is critical to begin identifying business interests in the beginning of their career and establish a process to educate, research, and explore how to invest and make money in a business opportunity. For certain players this may take years, depending on their sense of urgency. Others may dive right into the process. Nevertheless, it is imperative to understand the process and spend the necessary time to review business opportunities from a clear perspective. Considering the risk and time commitment, you want to make sure the opportunity is something you find interesting and something that fits your long-term business planning objectives.

Rule 2: Work with your advisory team to conduct a thorough analysis of any business deal or investment opportunity.

I think it is imperative to prepare professional athletes for life after sports. The urgency of this process is different for each person, especially when you consider the player's contract. Developing a plan and working to educate yourself on how to achieve success upon retirement is critical in order to manage risks and maximize opportunities. Make sure you have the tools and the confidence to succeed from the beginning of your career.

Oftentimes, athletes fail to set up their financial, tax, and estate plans prior to exploring business opportunities. This is a mistake since it is imperative that you understand how to evaluate business opportunities in light of risk tolerance, budget, tax planning, and long-term financial objectives. Once these items are addressed, the next step is to evaluate each business proposal with detail and care. A careful and thorough analysis of every facet of the proposal, from background checks of key players to a review of all financial statements, tax issues, legal documents, market analysis, and your financial situation, is essential.

Because a business investment typically is considered an illiquid investment, an investor needs to be comfortable with the fact that they may not see a penny of profit for several years. This may be hard for you if you are not used to looking toward the long run and want to see immediate returns. Another issue to consider is whether you want to be a "silent" investor (not personally involved in the company) or an "active" investor (actively growing and involved in the company from management to tasks). The answers to these questions will help you and your advisors determine which business opportunities you should consider.

An important and often overlooked factor to consider before investing in a business opportunity is your personal goals and interests. It may be that you enjoy real estate or have always wanted to own a beer distributorship. Some athletes are interested in the entertainment business. I know certain athletes who acquired a music studio and launched a record label, lost money, and tried to sell the business two years later without success. Sometimes you do things just to do them, and if you lose money, that's okay—so long as from the day you invest your first penny, you know the odds of making a profit are slim and you don't jeopardize your future lifestyle needs.

It is critical to make sure the right people or teams review your business proposals. Most of the time, it's not your investment advisor or your agent. Rather, you need to hire a team of business consultants who are seasoned experts in business plan evaluations, banking, financial modeling, competitive analysis, and knowledge of a variety of industries—and who do not have a conflict. Typically, investment advisors are not trained to advise in such a capacity, and they are not authorized by their company to do so. Also, investment advisors have an inherent conflict of interest since they make money off the money you invest with them. Thus, to the extent you withdraw money from your investment account to "fund" a business opportunity, you are essentially decreasing the investment advisor's fee income.

Your business consultants should be able to review pro formas, cash flow statements, balance sheets, and every other document related to the proposal, including whether as an investor you are going to be obligated to invest more money if the company issues a capital call and to what extent you would be liable for company debt issued by a bank upon loan default. These are critical issues! Your team also needs to know how to tear apart a company's accounting records, lawsuits, or other liabilities and reveal any financial or material weaknesses. They should absorb data and prepare an investment summary that an athlete is able to review and understand in order to make an independent decision as to whether or not they should start or invest in the business opportunity.

Upon completion of the business analysis, you will find that most deals are not cut-and-dried. Usually such an analysis explains, "This could be a good deal if they do x, y, and z," or "You could lose all your money if d, e, and f happen." Assuming the basic fundamentals of the business pass the due diligence evaluation, most deals come down to the success of the management team or technology behind the business.

Many athletes make a critical error in failing to engage a specific business consultant. Typically, the athlete relies upon the individual who presented the deal—a financial advisor or a family member, for instance— to provide the analysis. It's best if you engage a qualified, independent, third-party advisor to review deals in order to avoid the potential for a conflict of interest when either your agent or investment advisor introduces you to a deal. The deal may be well worth the investment, but that conclusion should come from an independent advisor who is qualified to conduct an analysis and who does not stand to benefit financially if you decide to invest.

An independent review will cost money—potentially thousands of dollars, in most cases. But a review under that format breeds accountability and will more often than not save you money and bring peace of mind. Most clients would rather spend $2,000–$5,000 to make sure they don't lose $500,000 or $1 million or more. I have experienced many examples of how a relatively small fee paid to qualified advisors has saved clients millions of otherwise lost dollars.

Another important factor to consider as to why a business consultant is a critical hire in order to evaluate a deal is when that consultant is able to negotiate a better deal for the athlete because of the advisor's independence and detailed understanding of the transaction. Since a professional athlete is recognizable in certain markets, the use of an athlete's name and likeness to either market a business or attract other investors in a business can be valuable. As a result, additional consideration in the form of more ownership, potential income, control, or otherwise should be negotiated to compensate an athlete accordingly.

Unless you pay a team of experienced professionals to review and negotiate terms of business deals, you will inevitably make the same mistakes that cost Brooks and Boselli in their earlier years. The problem is that a professional review of any business opportunity takes time and money. Be mindful, however, that it is time and money well spent and will help you sleep better at night, knowing your investments have been given a green light by professionals. "Paying an advisor to review my business deals would have been the greatest return on investment I'd ever had if I'd done it in the beginning," Boselli says.[4]

Rule 3: Trust your instincts.

Do not forget to trust your instincts. Looking back on his failed business venture, Brooks says there were multiple signs that it was a bad deal. He and the other two investors wrote a large check to an account set up by the "promoter" (an individual who is arranging a business deal). Brooks and the other investors were to be listed on the account as well, in order to require the consent of all of the account holders before a check could be written from the account. The promoter cashed the check within twenty-four hours. Brooks went to the bank to see that the check had been cashed and money spent by the promoter, only to learn that he and the other investors were not listed on the account. Despite promises to add their names to the account, it never happened. Brooks caught him in one lie after another. "I saw the signs," he says. "But by the eighth, ninth, or tenth sign, the money was gone, and there was nothing we could do to recover."[5]

Your instincts are important. Most of us experience certain behavior or circumstances that should alert us as to whether someone is being truthful or whether we are not getting the full story. Sometimes these red flags can appear when asking to review documents and they are not provided or are incomplete, or even when someone seems hostile when asked to provide information relative to their business or background. There are a number of signs. Pay attention to them and trust your instincts.

Rule 4: Evaluate the potential effects of a business opportunity with respect to your public image.

Before a review of the financial forecast or terms of a business opportunity, your advisors should address whether your name should be attached to a particular project. Depending on the business, it can put a positive or negative spin on a player's public image, which stretches further than you might think.

Certain business investments may have the potential to generate significant income or value, but the nature of the business could threaten your ability to secure existing or future endorsements. Certain companies don't want a spokesman who is attached to the adult film industry, organized dogfighting, gambling, or industries that rely on child labor. It could also pose a threat to future contract negotiations if team management begins to see you and your business activities as a liability or distraction to the organization.

When an athlete reaches the professional level, there will always be a certain group of people who will try to find things wrong with you, and will try you in the court of public opinion for perceived or alleged biases, opinions, or beliefs. Your business activities are not exempt from such public scrutiny. Approach any business deals with a full understanding of the long-term ramifications they may pose to your public image and decide whether you're comfortable with the risk.

Rule 5: Consider the source.

Though business deals can be lucrative, some of my clients have lost big money through these arrangements because they have put their trust in strangers whom they believed to be trustworthy.

It is easy to be drawn in by a slick, fast-talking salesman. They are experts at convincing us they are good at what they do, and it is easy for us to be inspired and motivated by their sales pitches. Some are very good at it.

Equally threatening is a business deal with a friend or family member. You may think there is a built-in trust factor in those relationships, but each deal has to be approached with the same level of scrutiny.

Weeding through business deals and finding the right people to partner with can be stressful, because the people behind the deal are every bit as important as the financial viability of the arrangement. Always consider the origin of the deal and the motivations of those behind it.

Boselli says it is often difficult to look at the big picture because people often assume that others—family and friends, in particular—have their best interests at heart. That is true in some cases and not true in many cases. "We're human beings," he says. "We love people, and we trust people. And unfortunately, people take advantage of that, and we get into deals that aren't the best for us. That has happened to me."

Boselli's advice for young players? "Business is business, whether it's with your family, with a church member, with a teammate, or with your best friend. You need to treat every transaction like that. If you handle it that way and if you have people on your side looking into the deal, you will be protected in the long run. And actually, it will save your relationships and keep your relationships safe if you end up hiring someone independent who can be the bad guy when there needs to be a bad guy."

Boselli admits he made costly mistakes in the past and says he was young and naïve. He now approaches business deals with the assistance of a competent and reliable advisor with no stake in the deal, and has altered his own attitude toward business deals.

"I'm very cynical and negative when anybody brings me any kind of deal," he says. He has been able to look past personal relationships and predisposed feelings about an individual when it comes to business, and instead evaluates a deal based on its merits by hiring an independent business consulting team to evaluate the opportunity.[6]

Rule 6: Coordinate business planning with your estate plan.

When an athlete launches a new business or joins an existing ownership group, problems frequently surface due to a failure on the athlete's part to coordinate that business with his overall corporate and estate plan. Coordinating your business planning with your legal team ensures the corporate structure of those business investments are in compliance with the goals and objectives of your estate plan and can shield your other assets from liability associated with the business opportunity. For example, if you buy an apartment building in order to rent out the apartments to tenants as an investment and the building burns down, injuring or killing various tenants, you will get sued. If you didn't set up a company to own the apartment building, then your personal assets such as your stocks, bonds, and cash are all accessible to a creditor to satisfy the judgment in the event you are found liable by a judge or jury. However, if the apartment is owned by a company, then the creditor can't reach your personal assets to satisfy the judgment (there a few legal exceptions) and you contain the liability to the company only.

In far too many cases, very little thought is put into forming a company under an appropriate tax structure, whether that is a Limited Liability Company (LLC), an S corporation (a type of corporation that elects to have the income generated taxed at the individual level, thus avoiding the double taxation associated with traditional corporations), a partnership, an international company, or one of a number of other options. I often suggest holding companies for clients to operate and manage their various business operations. A holding company is a company set up to own and manage other subsidiary companies. Typically, you will own the holding company personally through another company or trust. Major goals of a holding company structure are to coordinate management of operations, maximize tax efficiencies, and provide for asset protection of the various business interests and the future opportunity to shift taxable wealth to your family or nonprofits in an efficient fashion.

Your advisors should know how to determine what course of action is necessary to protect your assets from another partner's bankruptcy or from potential creditors if that partner or coinvestor is subject to financial distress outside of the business investment. If a business partner doesn't have enough money to pay his or her portion of the debt, your advisors should work to protect your interests from further exposure. Many of these details are handled through the various legal documents initially drafted to set up the company. It is imperative you ask the following questions before entering into business with someone:

- Was a background check and credit report performed on all shareholders, members, or partners in the deal?
- Are any of the shareholders, members, or partners in litigation or faced with pending lawsuits? This information may be obtained by resourceful private investigators or by simply asking. If the partners lie to you regarding this matter, you may be able to sue them for damages in the future.

- Did someone review whether the company's valuation is supported and reasonable in order to justify the percentage of the company you will own based on your investment?
- Was a marketplace analysis performed?
- Under the legal documents, what happens to a shareholder's, member's, or partner's interest if they file personal bankruptcy or are forced into involuntary bankruptcy?
- Under the legal documents, what happens to a shareholder's, member's, or partner's interest if they die or become disabled? Will you be in business with their spouse, children, or trusts?
- If legal documents include a buy-sell agreement (where the business or partners would be obligated to buy out the disabled or deceased partner's interest from his or her spouse, children, or trusts), how is that future obligation to be financed? From profits, life insurance, or some other means?
- Who is in control of the company? Who can control whether to borrow money, legally bind the company to any agreements, amend the legal documents, terminate the business, remove a partner, or mandate more money needs to be invested into the company?
- What happens if a partner cannot pay a capital call (invest more money into the company for debts, acquisitions, expenses, etc.)? If you cover someone else's capital call, how can you protect or secure repayment of the advance?
- How should you own your interest in the company? Through your holding company? Other?
- Are you protected from having to invest future money into the company if either you don't have the money at that time or the business is failing?
- Does the company have any existing or pending lawsuits?

- Are disputes among shareholders, members, or partners handled either in court or arbitration?
- Which state law will govern the terms of the formation documents? Wyoming, Florida, Delaware, or another state? Why is a certain state selected? Keep in mind, certain states afford higher levels of asset protection for members of an LLC or partners in a partnership than others.
- Who will keep all of the original business formation and ancillary documents? Who will make sure to keep up with various formalities and filings of the business to ensure good standing?

As you can see, the above questions require that you have a qualified attorney and business consultant looking out for you. Financial planners, investment advisors, and agents typically are not trained or qualified to handle these technical legal, tax, and business issues. More importantly, they do not have the time to handle such investments. Make sure to hire independent and experienced team members to structure and review all the above business issues when considering whether to invest in a business opportunity.

Rule 7: Don't be a cowboy.

Unfortunately, many athletes who suffer financial loss from failed business opportunities did not engage a third party to review the financial, legal, and tax issues associated with the opportunity. This is not to say that a business opportunity won't still fail even if the deal was reviewed and negotiated by a qualified team of advisors. At least under these circumstances, there is a better chance that the risks will be identified up front and the athlete will go into the deal knowing the risks. However, far too often, athletes engage in "cowboy deals," running off and signing onto a business deal without ever consulting the right type of advisor. Hiring a business advisor will cost the athlete money, and you may not like the recommendations. But you will save money down the road by avoiding bad deals and negotiating better terms for promising deals.

Keep in mind: neither the investor nor the advisors hired to evaluate a business opportunity have a crystal ball to help forecast which deal will work and which one will fail. There are key elements to any deal that should be reviewed before deciding whether to invest money or guarantee debt. Once these basic items are negotiated, the decision to move forward really comes down to whether the opportunity is just an "investment" or whether it is part of a larger business development plan to build long-term value, experience, relationships, and strategic positioning of a larger business initiative.

The experience and education an athlete will gain by consulting and discussing the business opportunity with his business consultant will not only serve to educate and inform the athlete about a number of issues in determining whether to invest in a business, but will also serve to keep the business opportunities coordinated with the athlete's financial plan so long-term objectives are not compromised when diverting dollars to outside business investments.

Chapter 6

Acquire a Passion for Charity

I have spent a significant amount of time in recent years managing the planned giving process on behalf of my clients. By organizing and overseeing some sizable financial gifts, helping form and grow clients' private foundations and public charities, and helping clients define and identify their charitable motivations, I have developed a strong appreciation for the power of giving back and leaving a legacy.

The power of planned giving—a process that facilitates charitable giving by a donor during his or her life or upon their death—is extremely moving, and yet it is something that not many people ever experience.

In my initial discussions with a professional athlete, I share my belief that a successful professional athlete has the opportunity to extend their legacy beyond the field of play and leave a significant impact on their community or the lives of others. It is not easy for certain athletes who are young and not used to having significant wealth to consider the impact they can have by dedicating their time or financial resources for a cause that is meaningful to them. While I believe that it is difficult to effectively take care of others if you haven't first taken care of yourself, helping others can help you better yourself and improve your self-confidence and sense of purpose.

I believe everyone has a moral responsibility to give back to the community in a meaningful way and should try to leave a legacy through planned giving. Not all of us have access to the financial resources to leave large amounts of money to an organization or write a large check every year to our favorite charity. Additionally, many of us don't have the time to dedicate to such causes. However, successful professional athletes have something many of us don't have—the power of celebrity. Whether or not an athlete contributes a dime to a particular cause may be less relevant than he or she championing a cause. A notable athlete will attract media attention and, with proper management, inspire and motivate others to support a cause either financially or with their time.

The following rules will help athletes decide how to give back and how to integrate their charity efforts alongside their professional and financial journey in an effort to maximize the experience.

Rule 1: Tap into your passions.

When I discuss with a client the various ways through which he can give back to his community, financially or through the gift of time, I ask him to share with me his passions. This can be difficult, however, because at a young age, you don't always know what charitable missions you are passionate about. Perhaps an athlete cares deeply about a particular cause, such as cancer research and awareness, or wants to champion efforts to benefit the citizens of an impoverished country or community. But just as often, it hasn't crossed his mind to be concerned about the rest of the world, or he isn't sure how to manage the process and develop a process and approach that is meaningful.

An athlete's sentiments toward planned giving are often a result of their upbringing and personal experiences. The key issue is to plant the seed of nonprofit planning as soon as possible so the athlete will begin to think about how he or she wants to impact others.

I try to educate my clients about the various outlets to which they can direct their money and volunteer efforts. This process involves exposing athletes to many diverse opportunities. For example, I took one pro athlete on a tour of a children's hospital, not for the purpose of soliciting money, but to show him that a hospital is not just bricks and mortar, but rather a place filled with children whose stories can be heartbreaking and uplifting. On another occasion, I presented a client with an opportunity to help build a basketball academy in Africa. Several years ago, I introduced an athlete to a microfinance program that helps finance small business loans to the underprivileged and disadvantaged.

Clients have been touched by all types of experiences and often find a cause they can adopt from the process. Some athletes have spent time learning about well-known philanthropists such as Andrew Carnegie and Warren Buffet and the effect that their charitable work has had across the country and around the world. Buffet's multibillion-dollar pledge to the Bill and Melinda Gates Foundation was both legendary and inspiring not only because of the dollar amount, but because the act of giving away that level of wealth forces others to reconsider the true meaning of success and our own perception of the value of wealth-building.

Is success working tirelessly for generations to afford a nice lifestyle and then leaving your fortune to your family in hopes that they will lead a productive and fulfilling life? Or rather is success working for generations to afford a nice lifestyle and then leaving your fortune to charity with the hope that your gift will transform others and improve the outcome of your cause? Maybe success is a combination of both. In any event, those with access to celebrity and wealth have a tremendous opportunity to build a legacy for generations to come. Sometimes all it takes is to be inspired and touched.

It is critical that an athlete explore charitable planning seriously and at every level of their playing career. Unless an athlete has initiated the charitable journey on their own, their advisors should help introduce the possibilities and personal satisfaction of charitable planning. Of course, there are athletes who simply don't care about planned giving or are too busy with their own lives to give it any consideration. However, I challenge all clients who seem to dismiss the power of charity and philanthropy to visit a community center, supported by charitable giving, or a children's hospital, which relies on charity to operate and provide medical and emotional support to patients and their families, or to visit a research facility working on a cure for ALS. They come away with a much higher respect for the power of charity and the impact it has on communities and individual lives.

Rule 2: Establish a foundation or charity.

Creating a private foundation or public charity is a popular tool to establish a managed and coordinated effort to facilitate charitable contributions. A private foundation is a nonprofit organization that derives its funding and support from an individual, family, or business and usually distributes those funds through grants to other charitable organizations. A public charity differs in that, as a nonprofit, it derives its funding and support from the general public. Determining which type of nonprofit to apply for depends on where the funds to support your nonprofit will come from and how those funds will be spent. If an athlete plans to provide the financial support for the foundation and devote at least 65 percent of the foundation's assets to tax-exempt activity, then private foundation status is likely the choice. On the other hand, if an athlete plans to solicit funds from the general public through fundraisers or other activities to be spent on charitable causes, then organizing as a public charity may be favorable.

Derrick Brooks's charity, Derrick Brooks Charities Inc., was created when he was approached about donating football game tickets to a group of children. It has grown into an organization that works to provide educational opportunities for at-risk youth. Brooks has become passionate about the mission of his foundation and has inspired other athletes to follow a similar path.

When someone of influence sets a trend related to planned giving, it validates and inspires others to consider their own planned giving efforts. Younger players can see the difference that experienced athletes have made in their communities and witness the benefits they have reaped in exchange. For example, some of my veteran clients have leveraged the business contacts they met through their charity work to create consulting opportunities. In one case, an NFL client was able to generate over $35,000 per month by simply agreeing to introduce a certain business to high-level prospective clients. This opportunity to supplement the athlete's monthly income was the direct result of his charity work and the time he spent developing relationships in the community through his nonprofit experience.

While forming a private foundation or public charity is relatively simple, managing such an organization requires more time than just the few minutes one takes sending money every year to a local United Way chapter. The challenge is to identify a mission or message and pursue that mission or message with clarity, purpose, and urgency. "If you don't believe in the message, then don't start a foundation," Brooks tells young athletes. "You don't need money to start a foundation," he says. "You need time."[1]

Private foundations also allow many athletes to incorporate their brand in order to expand their marketability, create business relationships outside of sports, and enhance their relationship within a community. Many of my clients have realized the multiple benefits from a private foundation or public charity. However, experienced and qualified foundation management is absolutely critical to ensure a successful experience. There are many organizations and people who specialize in nonprofit management. Be careful of those who claim they can handle this service, yet have no track record, staff, or sophisticated nonprofit experience. As for any other advisor, make sure you interview several organizations, check references, and conduct background checks.

Rule 3: Give the gift of time.

Many people forget how valuable and influential the gift of one's time is as opposed to the gift of money. Brooks's passion for charitable work did not grow out of his financial contributions, but out of his time spent with children. When he made that first step and purchased football tickets for a group of children, he not only donated the tickets but met face-to-face with them, realizing he would have a greater effect on those children if he sat down and talked to them about school. He discovered that the innocence of children allowed him to intervene and have a lasting effect on their lives. "You don't feel your time is wasted," he says.[2]

Brooks was a central figure in the construction of Brooks-DeBartolo Collegiate High School, a public charter school that opened in 2007 in Tampa Bay, Florida, where at-risk youth receive private educational opportunities. Rather than just writing a check to fund construction, he contributed a great deal of his personal time and effort to the project, seeing it through from conception to the point of being fully operational.

It was a huge undertaking, and something for which he will always be remembered.

Playing basketball with a disadvantaged youth, playing video games with a sick child, listening to the struggles of a single parent with children, or simply presenting the need for further research to advance a cure for ALS in many ways may have a stronger impact long-term than simply writing a check. Time is valuable and should never be discounted or underestimated. As we become more successful and our lives more complex, it becomes easier to write checks for our causes in order to satisfy our conscience. However, we cannot forget the impact, value, and lasting impression we could have on others by simply spending our time promoting our message or purpose.

Rule 4: Take advantage of the benefits afforded through planned giving.

As a professional athlete, you should become involved in planned giving for the right reason: a desire to leave the world a better place than you found it. But also realize that your involvement can benefit your tax and estate planning efforts as well as your business endeavors. A cash donation to any charitable organization, including a private foundation, is tax deductible. Tax deductions can reduce the taxes one owes to the IRS.

Some athletes also direct a portion of their estates to their foundations or charities upon death. Such planning is a powerful testament to the athlete's commitment to their legacy, but also may reduce their taxable estate, thus saving significant money and preserving more for their family, assuming they are subject to estate taxes.

Some individuals faced with a considerable estate tax leave their entire estate to their private foundation or a charity. In some instances, that plan provides an opportunity for a family member—a child, perhaps—to run the foundation as a salaried employee. This can be an effective strategy to provide your family reasonable compensation for running the foundation or charity, keep them involved in the legacy you worked to build, and at the same time reduce the amount of estate tax owed to the IRS.

An athlete's planned giving efforts will build a great deal of goodwill in his community, family, team, and sponsors. People want to be affiliated with those who give back to the community. An athlete's financial and volunteer contributions serve to benefit not only the community, but those who are looking to be inspired as well. By attending fundraisers, meeting other philanthropists, and developing relationships with community-minded businesses, my clients have had many doors opened to new opportunities.

The ultimate reward for the athlete varies, but for Brooks his charitable work rewards him in a bit simpler way: "To see the smiles on kids' faces." He says his involvement with youth saved him from many of the negative influences that can affect young pros. At the end of the day, rather than heading out for happy hour, Brooks went to the Boys and Girls Club to watch a football game and spend time with children. "It gave me a sense of focus that was different from the other influences that were available at the time," he says. "That's why I say, 'Y'all saved me.'"[3]

Afterword

For mothers and fathers, brothers and sisters, and other close family and friends, witnessing a loved one's athletic success at the amateur level and emergence into the national spotlight is an experience that serves as a great source of pride. It is a journey that can be enjoyed and experienced not just by the athlete but by his entire family.

The bright lights of fame and fortune can be blinding, however, and families can also get caught up in the magical whirlwind of the experience and fail to acknowledge a critical fact: Most athletes will not go on to play professional sports. If they do, their career may be short-lived. For many, that means their playing days are over by their twenty-sixth birthday. Athletes and their families don't emphasize the value of those years because no one wants to admit it may be that short—shorter if the athlete gets hurt.

In addition, many athletes and their families fall victim to the belief that he or she is going to be the best athlete of all time. To think otherwise is believed to be a sign of weakness, and any shadow of a doubt compromises an athlete's ability to succeed on the playing field—or so they believe.

However, if athletes approach the opportunity to play professional sports with the right perspective, their journeys will have the potential to completely change their lives and the lives of their family members now and in future generations. Balancing the success, staying true to your roots and identity, supporting your community, prioritizing you family and friends, and being responsible with your wealth are key elements to making the most of the opportunity to play professional sports.

Keep in mind, at some point every athlete voluntarily or involuntarily retires and is no longer employed. Thus, it is important to enjoy the ride and work hard, but don't turn a blind eye to the reality of the situation. The journey will end at one point, and the rest of your life will be before you. Many relationships will slowly wind down once your career is over. However, the most important relationships—those with your children, spouse, parents, friends, your community, and yourself—will take on even greater importance. Make sure to prepare yourself for the transition so that you can successfully engage in those relationships and succeed in all aspects, despite no longer making as much money, no longer being sought after by fans and the media, and no longer hearing the crowd roar when your name is announced before a game or match.

"Most of these athletes think it's never going to end," Tony Boselli says. "The inherent problem is these guys go from having no money to having millions of dollars overnight, and it's like they won the lotto."[1]

Younger athletes have a more difficult time understanding the long run. For advisors, that is difficult to observe because we preach the importance of proper planning for the long term.

"At the end of the day, it's a business," Boselli says. "You're an entity, you're a corporation, and your athletic ability is a major asset. You need to protect that, and you need to watch out for that and realize that as soon as that asset loses value or no longer provides any value to the team, it will no longer be wanted. And that's just the reality of professional sports in this country."[2]

I hope that this book can provide athletes and their families with some insight and direction related to successfully navigating their career and financial opportunities. Having worked with athletes at the highest level from all the perspectives mentioned in this book, I can state without a doubt that it is a privilege to work alongside some of the best in the business and witness their growth and evolution as fathers, husbands, athletes, businessmen, and community leaders. My mission is to hopefully connect with you as a reader at some level with respect to the contents of this book. If I can help prevent an athlete from being taken advantage of or from making a business mistake, or if I can help that athlete realize an opportunity, organize their wealth planning objectives, or save money, then I have met my personal objective by sharing my experiences and those of my clients in this book. Sports are entertainment, and an athlete's participation as part of that entertainment should be limited to their performance on the field during their career. Commit to your financial, business, tax, and legal matters off the field with the same discipline you approach your on-the-field performance with.

By understanding the above chapters and listening to lessons learned from veteran players, you will improve the odds of maximizing and protecting your income as a professional athlete in order to support your lifestyle and family long after your playing career has ended.

Endnotes

Chapter 1—How to Blend Fame and Money with Family

1. Quote from telephone interview with Derrick Brooks.
2. Quote from telephone interview with Derrick Brooks.
3. Quote from telephone interview with Derrick Brooks.
4. Quote from telephone interview with Eric Steinbach.
5. 26 USC §2505.
6. Quotes from telephone interview with Tony Boselli.

Chapter 2—Consider the Value of Spirituality

1. Quotes from telephone interview with Derrick Brooks.
2. Quote from telephone interview with Tony Boselli.
3. Quote from telephone interview with Tony Boselli.
4. Quotes from telephone interview with Derrick Brooks.
5. Smith, Gary. "The Chosen One," *Sports Illustrated*, Dec. 23, 1996.
6. Thamel, Pete. "Tebow Returning to Florida for Final Year," *New York Times*, Jan. 11, 2009.
7. Quotes from telephone interview with Derrick Brooks.
8. Quotes from telephone interview with Tony Boselli.
9. Derived from telephone interview with Eric Steinbach.

Chapter 3—Build a Winning Team of Advisors

1. Quote from telephone interview with Derrick Brooks.
2. Quote from telephone interview with Tony Boselli.
3. Quote from telephone interview with Derrick Brooks.
4. Quotes from telephone interview with Tony Boselli.
5. Quote from telephone interview with Eric Steinbach.
6. Derived from telephone interview with Derrick Brooks.
7. Quote from telephone interview with Tony Boselli.
8. Quote from telephone interview with Tony Boselli.

Chapter 4—Use Wealth Planning to Secure Your Future

1. Economic Growth and Tax Relief Reconciliation Act of 2001 (EGTRRA).
2. Bernard Madoff was convicted of running a fraudulent investment operation that paid returns to investors from other investors' funds rather than from actual profits. Investors lost billions. Robert Allen Stanford, chairman of the Stanford Financial Group, also became the subject of a fraud investigation in 2009.
3. Quotes from telephone interview with Eric Steinbach.
4. Quote from telephone interview with Derrick Brooks.
5. Quote from telephone interview with Tony Boselli.
6. Quotes from telephone interview with Tony Boselli.

Chapter 5—Identify Your Best Options in Business Opportunities

1. Derived from telephone interview with Derrick Brooks.
2. Derived from telephone interview with Tony Boselli.
3. Quote from telephone interview with Derrick Brooks.

4. Quote from telephone interview with Tony Boselli.
5. Quote from telephone interview with Derrick Brooks.
6. Quotes from telephone interview with Tony Boselli.

Chapter 6—Acquire a Passion for Charity

1. Quote from telephone interview with Derrick Brooks.
2. Quote from telephone interview with Derrick Brooks.
3. Quote from telephone interview with Derrick Brooks.

Afterword

1. Quote from telephone interview with Tony Boselli.
2. Quote from telephone interview with Tony Boselli.

Additional Resources

Web sites

https://www.kiplinger.com/
http://www.mymoney.gov/
http://www.smartaboutmoney.org/
www.napfa.org

Books

Adkisson, Jay, and Chris Riser. *Asset Protection: Concepts and Strategies for Protecting Your Wealth*. New York: McGraw-Hill, 2004.

Clifford, Denis. *Estate Planning Basics*. Berkeley, CA: NOLO, 2007.

Kansas, Dave. *The Wall Street Journal Complete Money and Investing Guidebook*. New York: Three Rivers Press, 2005.

Kelly, Jason. *The Neatest Little Guide to Stock Market Investing*. New York: Plume, 2007.

Kobliner, Beth. *Get a Financial Life: Personal Finance in Your Twenties and Thirties.* 3rd ed. New York: Fireside, 2009.

Kristof, Kathy. *Investing 101.* New York: Bloomberg Press, 2008.

Silk, Roger D., James W. Lintott, Andrew R. Stephens, and Christine M. Silk. *Creating a Private Foundation: The Essential Guide for Donors and Their Advisors.* Princeton: Bloomberg Press, 2003.